Costumes, Accessories, Props, and Stage Illusions Made Easy

Barb Rogers

MERIWETHER PUBLISHING LTD.
Colorado Springs, Colorado

Meriwether Publishing Ltd., Publisher
P.O. Box 7710
Colorado Springs, CO 80933

Editor: Theodore O. Zapel
Assistant Editor: Dianne Bundt
Cover and book design: Jan Melvin
Interior illustrations: Jan Melvin
Interior photography: Barb Rogers

Library of Congress Cataloging-in-Publication Data

Rogers, Barb, 1947-
    Costumes, accessories, props, and stage illusions made easy / Barb Rogers.
       p. cm.
    Includes bibliographical references and index.
    ISBN-10: 1-56608-103-3
    ISBN-13: 978-1-56608-103-0
      1. Costume. 2. Clothing and dress--Remaking. 3. Vintage clothing. I. Title.
    TT633.R636 2005
    646.4'78--dc22
                              2005004359

    1   2   3   05   06   07

Dedication

To those who have crossed over but had so much impact on my life,
who taught me how to survive, who loved me in spite of myself.
In loving memory of:

My son, Ron, not long on the earth, but forever in my heart;
my mother, Charline Chaplin, who taught me what not to settle for;
and Roberta and Syd Doty, Glen Rodgers, Marcella Rodgers,
Jim Ralston, Bob Hartman, Fern Brannon, Ellen McMillan, Roy Chaplin,
Juanita Kibler, Bob and Ruth Poffinbarger, Connie Chaplin,
and my special friend, Helen Wright

Acknowledgments

I would like to extend a special thank you to all those people who have given me so much love and support — and old clothes.

Mickey Gaines and Connie Adams, dear friends who always bail me out;

Cheryl Robinson, who has been with me since the beginning;

Ruth Belden, my friend through good times and bad;

Katy Harrison, another diamond in the rough;

Cindy Daly, a wonderful, giving neighbor and friend;

Tom and Jacqui McKibben, who will always be our special friends;

my sisters and brothers-in-law: Roslyn Hartman, Wanda and Jim LaBounty, Joan Ralston, Don Rodgers, and Molly and Mickey Rogers;

Jennifer Walsh, a beautiful person inside and out;

Susan Powell Miller and Regina Juarez, my Maui buddies;

Donna Gordon and Max, there would be a hole in my life without you two;

Nancy Bruns and Jim Walker, who feed me well;

my very special nieces: Susan Tibbits, Julia Pendersen, Gala Kimberlin, Crystal Brasil, and Susan Hartman;

and to my husband, the love of my life who knows me better than I know myself. Thank you for your love, support, and patience.

Contents

Preface

Many of the costumes and accessories included in this book were made over the years and have found a home in rental shops and theatre companies and are used year after year to enhance parade floats and masquerade parties.

Using the conversion method, you too can create fabulous, unique costumes for your needs with very little money, time, or expertise. You don't need to be a seamstress to make a costume. You just need an imagination and the willingness to hunt the thrift shops, garage sales, and discount stores for that perfect item you can convert into a costume. Think simply and have fun.

It's always more fun in costume, so whether you're looking for a full costume or a hat or mask to accessorize your own clothing, I hope you'll think of my methods and use them to keep it fast, cheap, and easy.

Introduction

I am an illusionist. Using everyday clothing — something that has been discarded — I do magic, transforming otherwise common people into superheroes, movie stars, knights, and other extraordinary characters. You see, people in search of a costume don't care how you get the desired effect; they merely want to look the part.

Costuming is in the details. The exact same garment can take on a totally different look depending on how you accessorize it. Take a long-sleeved, full-length black dress as an example. Put a cape, pointed hat, and broom with it, and you have a witch. Put a white collar, apron, and black and white bonnet with it, and you have a pilgrim. Cut some holes and add a belt, chains, fabric paint, and small hat with a drape, and you have gone medieval. You are only limited by your imagination. The black dress is the canvas, and you are the artist.

Props also help determine the effect. Sit a man in a chair, and he is just a man in a chair. Convert the chair into a throne, and he is a king. Put a man in an overcoat and he's simply another man. Add a fedora and gun, and he becomes menacing. Props help set the mood of the costume.

An illusion costume is one that is not what it appears to be. You've seen them: the man who looks as if he's riding a horse, the clown car that is actually strapped to the clown underneath his costume, even a headless man carrying a severed head on a platter. Are these difficult to make? Not if you think simple.

A teacher once told me I had a tendency to take everything down to its simplest form and that such a tendency would not serve me well in life. Everyone's entitled to his opinion, but in costuming it has served me quite well. I could have learned to sew, use patterns, and go through the painstaking process of making costumes, hats, and accessories ... but why, when there is an easier way? The clothing manufacturer has already done all the mundane work, so I get to have fun with it.

Earlier in my costuming career, I had very little money or time. Even if I'd known where to buy my accessories, I wouldn't have been able to afford them. But a trip to the thrift shops, a day rummaging at garage sales, and sometimes even a walk past people's garbage cans would bring me the treasures I needed to turn that old dress, suit, or robe into a fabulous costume. Actually, I began to enjoy the thrill of the hunt, and the way my heart stood still when they told me it was only two dollars. Before I got the item home, I was redesigning it, making the accessories in my mind that would transform it into something magical.

As my business grew from one room to fifteen and my costuming time grew limited, I found easier, faster, and cheaper ways to make things. Many times there was no time to hunt; I had to make accessories with whatever was at hand. They say necessity is the mother of invention, but lack of time will produce the same results. When I'm in a hurry, it isn't unusual for me to grab a shoulder pad out of a garment, add a tie, decorate it, and turn it into a hat. That is how I've discovered some of my best, and certainly my most unique and creative, work.

In this book, I will share with you all the secrets I've learned over the years. Imagine turning the sleeves of a robe into leggings; a shirt yoke into Cleopatra's collar; a suit into a frock cat, military uniform, cutaway, even a matador. I'll help you understand why it is better to purchase feathers and sequins to make your own masks rather than buy pre-made ones. I'll show you how to change cheap cardboard hats into wonderful creations, straw into gold (as far as costuming is concerned), and cheap plastic masks into unbelievable, unique designs that will last. (Yes, I can make plastic bend.) We will do beading without beads and create fabulous jewelry from collars, dress bodices, and Christmas trim. These things and more I will teach you — in my own simple way.

As long as you don't complicate the process, anyone should be able to make a wonderful costume using my methods. Get rid of your old ideas, open your mind, believe you can do it, and half the battle is over. Because you don't have to go through the work of making costumes and accessorizing from scratch, costuming should be a, creative process, filled with the childlike glory of playing pretend. There are no rules, so do it however it works. And most importantly, have a good time. Costumes should be fun — not only for the wearer, but also for the designer.

Materials

Glue and Scissors

Other than your imagination, the two most important tools you will need to complete projects from this book are a glue gun and a good, sharp pair of scissors. There are many types of glue guns, ranging from cool melt to hot glue guns. After much research and many burns, I've chosen the Magic Melt Glue Gun purchased from Red Hill Adhesives. (See the reference section at the back of the book.) I buy my glue by the pound in ten-inch sticks so I don't have to continually feed the glue gun. Magic Melt glue is the best I've used and holds well after washing.

I normally keep two pairs of scissors — one cheaper, heavy-duty pair to cut cardboard, hats, straw, and plastic; and a really good sharp pair for fabric. If you use your fabric shears for other things, you will ruin them. If you use dull scissors for fabric, it will be an exercise in agony; the fabric will catch and pull and the look will not be neat.

Sculptural Arts Coating

For many of my accessories and props (anything that won't need washing) I use Sculptural Arts Coating (see the reference section to find out where to purchase). Sculptural Arts Coating is a white, paste-like product that dries clear and remains flexible. It can be bought in many quantities, and anyone can buy it, but only through the company listed in the reference section.

Paint

Because we will be making a lot of props, we need to talk about paint. Spray paints are good for big projects, but for smaller props, I like the metallic brush-on paints. At our local hardware store, I can buy Plasti-Kote Odds 'n' Ends Fast Dry Enamel. This has to be one of the best paints I've ever used. Many times I have sequin appliques I've removed from gowns, but they are the wrong color for the costume I'm making. I paint them with gold leaf, silver, even copper enamel, and it covers great. You can't tell the sequins were ever another color. You won't believe how much time and money this paint will save you.

Fabric paint will also save you a lot of time. I used to spend hours beading costumes, such as Native American clothes, by hand, but now I use drops of fabric paint to create the illusion of beading. Before I discovered fabric paint, it might have taken me days to complete a beaded project; now it takes an hour. The fabric paint is washable and you eliminate the possibility that one thread will come loose and all your beads will fall off. Fabric paint is easy to find, inexpensive to buy, and anyone can use it. It can be painted on with a brush, dropped on for beads, or applied in lines — however you need to use it.

Finding Bargains

Depending on the type of project you're doing, you will be searching thrift shops, garage sales, junk stores, perhaps through your closet or someone else's for the appropriate garments, hats, or prop materials you need. You must learn to look at things in a different way — not for what they are but for what they can become.

Trim

While on the hunt for what you need, keep your eye out for trim. Trim is anything that can be glued on to give you the look you want. I watch for bags of old jewelry. It doesn't matter if the jewelry is broken as long as it is cheap. And it doesn't matter if it's the wrong color; it can be painted. I also keep my eye out for bags of silk flowers at the discount stores. These flowers are the ones that fall off or get damaged. Retailers bag them up and sell them cheap. As you will see, I also use a lot of Christmas trim. If I can't find it at rummage sales, I wait till the day after Christmas and buy it on sale. You can get a lot of trim for very little money that way.

When I had a costume rental shop, I did business with two independent fabric shops in our town. They saved me the ends off the sequin ribbon and trim bolts. They kept a box under the counter and threw in the scraps. You would be amazed how much accumulated each month. When making accessories, sometimes one needs only a bit of glitz or trim. And fabric shops usually just throw it out anyway.

Keep your eye out for remnants at the discount stores. You can purchase some really nice fabric for next to nothing. And again, when making accessories, sometimes you only need a small piece. Many times, I buy old clothes just for the fabric, trim, or buttons. In particular, I watch for dresses with sequin appliques, beading, fringe, and when I'm lucky, beaded fringe. Of course, I have used beaded fringe off old lampshades or anything else I could find it on.

Besides beaded jewelry and Christmas beads, some of my best sources of beads are beaded curtains. They seem to be an item people buy and discard frequently at garage sales. They are a wonderful source of beads for showgirls, Cleopatras, and so on, and they are usually pretty cheap.

Wedding and cocktail dresses can also be a great source of trim, ruffles, sequin, and beaded appliques. With one wedding dress I can normally make one full costume and have enough trim and ruffle left over to decorate another costume. You will also be surprised how well wedding dresses dye. With the great new liquid dyes, it has become easier to mix colors to create the more unusual and antique looks you need.

If you can't find the trim you want in any of these ways, there is a trim and fabric shop listed in the reference section.

Feathers

Feathers — oh, how I love feathers! What they can do for a hat! And how would I make showgirls without them? Unfortunately, they're not as easy to find as trim. Some craft shops and discount stores carry them, which is great if you're doing one project, but if you are doing several and need a lot of feathers, buying them from such stores will get quite expensive. Sometimes I find feathers at rummage sales or on old hats; I even use the ones out of feather dusters. However, because I make so many things with feathers, I have a wonderful feather company to buy through. (See the reference section.) Through them, I can buy feathers by the pound — that's a lot of feathers. I can purchase bags of plumes in a variety of colors — strips of coque (rooster) feathers already strung and dyed. It's a feather person's paradise. Still, when I see feathers on anything cheap, I buy it whether I need it at the time or not. Sooner or later, I will use them. Feather boas are another source of feathers. They come in all levels of quality, and the price is equal to the quality. (See the reference section for where to buy both cheaper and more expensive boas.)

Asking Family and Friends

Another great resource for costume materials is your circle of friends and family. Let them know what you're doing. You might be surprised what they will come up with out of their closets, old trunks, or attics. I can't tell you how blessed I've been with friends and family. In fact, these days when they go rummaging, to auctions, or to thrift shops, they think of me and what I might need or want. I have been given some wonderful items.

Wherever you get the materials for your project, have fun in the process. Find those wonderful old things you can turn into the great costume and accessories you need. When you look at the final product, know that this is your creation and it was simple, cheap, and fun, and you made it yourself.

Section I

Costumes

Chapter 1 Full Costumes

In everyday life, people know they can take that basic black dress or a man's black suit, change the accessories, and make it look different. The same applies to costumes. Because my method of making costumes is very easy, cheap, and fast, I probably spend more time on the accessories that set off the costume than on the costume itself. I believe that details are what make the costume. Imagine Glenda without her crown. She'd just be another blond in a pink prom dress. Imagine Dorothy without those red slippers. How would she get home?

You get the idea. The point of this chapter is pulling it all together, taking an easy-to-make costume and turning it into a fictional character, a period piece, even an illusion.

Glenda

Glenda

One of my all-time favorite shows is *The Wizard of Oz,* and Glenda's costume is a classic. I created her costume using an old wedding dress, a piece of plastic, and the cardboard off of a pants hanger.

Making the Costume

1. Dye the wedding dress with bright pink dye. Put it through three wash cycles.

2. Cut the sleeves off at the shoulders. Cut them off again about six inches above the wrist. Glue silver sequins along the cut edges of the bottom portions. Discard the upper portion of the sleeves.

3. Cut the bottom net ruffle off the skirt. Glue it on at the shoulders to make short, puffy sleeves.

4. Bring the sides of the outer skirt up and pin them under to look like paniers.

5. Glue on silver sequins at the neckline and waist.

Glenda Original Garment

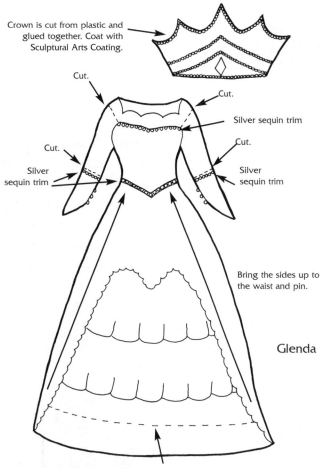

Crown is cut from plastic and glued together. Coat with Sculptural Arts Coating.

Cut.

Cut.

Silver sequin trim

Cut.

Cut.

Silver sequin trim

Silver sequin trim

Silver sequin trim

Bring the sides up to the waist and pin.

Glenda

Cut off bottom ruffle. Glue on shoulders to make puffy sleeves.

6. Coat a large piece of plastic from a poster frame with Sculptural Arts Coating and let it dry. Draw the tall crown on the plastic with a marker. Cut out the crown and glue the ends together at the back. Decorate it with pink and silver sequins and appliques.

7. To make the wand, glue pink sequins around the cardboard part of a pants hanger. Glue sequin applique on the end.

Glenda #2

There was another Glenda from *The Wiz,* an African-American version of the original. I loved her costumes. When making this Glenda, think more colorful, more impact with your costumes. I used a wedding dress and another dress that was given to me by friends to make this costume.

Glenda #2

Glenda #2
Original Garment #1
Wedding Dress

Making the Costume

1. Dye the wedding dress pink. Cut the train off so that the hem is even with the rest of the dress. Glue the hem under. Glue on a gold applique at the neckline.

2. Cut a triangular section from the back of the hot pink dress, a couple of inches below the zipper. The section will need to be large enough to cover the crown. (See step 5.) Glue the cut edges under.

3. Glue the fabric you cut from the train of the wedding dress around the waist of the hot pink dress and secure it with a gold applique in the center to create a panier look.

4. Put the hot pink dress over the wedding dress.

5. For the crown, glue the ends of a piece of foam together and cover it with the fabric from the back of hot pink dress. Coat with Sculptural Arts Coating. I glued beads from an old beaded curtain to the crown for decoration.

6. Make the neckpiece from a piece of pink lace trim glued to a ribbon that ties behind the neck.

7. Add a hoop skirt.

Glenda #2
Original Garment #2
Hot Pink Dress

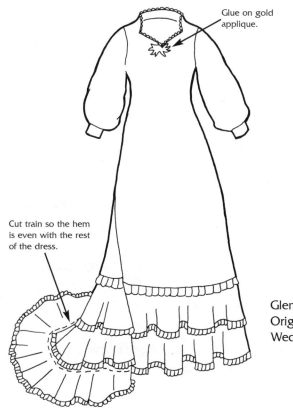

Glue on gold applique.

Cut train so the hem is even with the rest of the dress.

Glenda #2
Original Garment #1
Wedding Dress

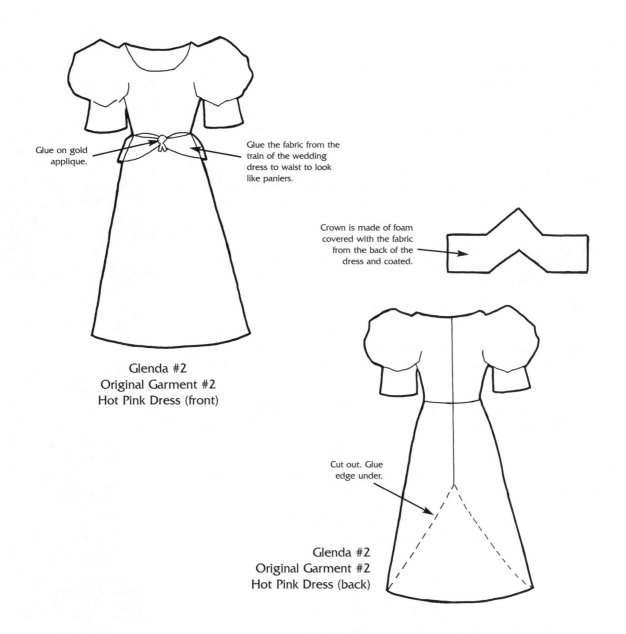

Glue on gold applique.

Glue the fabric from the train of the wedding dress to waist to look like paniers.

Crown is made of foam covered with the fabric from the back of the dress and coated.

Glenda #2
Original Garment #2
Hot Pink Dress (front)

Cut out. Glue edge under.

Glenda #2
Original Garment #2
Hot Pink Dress (back)

Yes, you can dye most wedding dresses. I've dyed hundreds of them. Be sure you wash them first, and leave the gown wet. Set the machine to the longest, hottest cycle. Add the dye and a half-cup of salt, then the garment. For a more brilliant color, stop the machine at the end of the wash cycle before the water drains and put the garment through more wash cycles until the desired color is achieved.

For instance, if you want a gray dress, use one bottle of black dye and put the garment through one cycle. If you want a bright orange dress, use three bottles of dye through three cycles. Do not simply let the garment soak in the dye. It needs to agitate to achieve full coverage. The salt will help the material absorb the dye. To dry, put the garment in the dryer on low or air fluff. The trim will normally dye darker than the dress because it is made of different material.

King

King

Making the Costume

1. Dye a white striped robe brown. The stripes will still show. Remove the tie belt.

2. Cut the hem of the robe to the desired length and cut off the sleeves, making the armholes larger to accommodate a man. Glue gold ruffled trim around the edges of the armholes and the hem.

3. Cut the arms and hem off of a purple robe, again making the armholes larger. Glue cut edges under.

4. To make the cape, cut the skirt off of a red dress. Glue the waist shut, fold the edge over, and glue. Fasten the skirt to the back of the striped robe with Velcro on both shoulders. Use wide Velcro for a more secure hold. You can also glue the skirt directly to the robe if you choose.

5. Put the purple robe over a white, full-sleeved blouse and a pair of red tights. Add a wide black belt with a large buckle.

6. Add a neck ruffle, a ruffle around the ankles that is connected with Velcro, a crown, and a scepter.

7. To make the crown, cover a piece of foam with purple fabric from the bottom of the robe and glue it inside a plastic crown so it shows between the points.

King
Original #1

King
Original #2

King
Original for cape

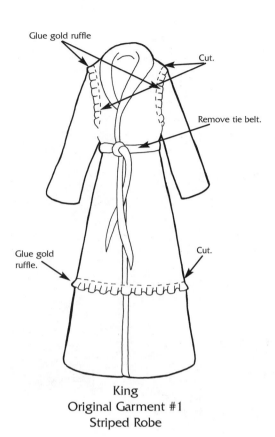

Glue gold ruffle

Cut.

Remove tie belt.

Glue gold ruffle.

Cut.

King
Original Garment #1
Striped Robe

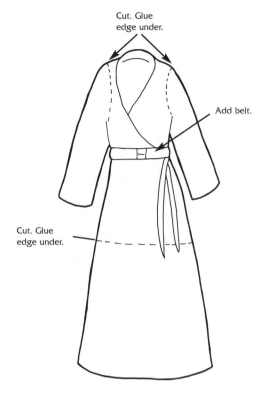

Cut. Glue edge under.

Add belt.

Cut. Glue edge under.

King
Original Garment #2
Purple Robe

Queen of Hearts

Queen of Hearts

Someone must have had a red and white wedding because I found two bright red bridesmaid dresses at the same place. One was ruffled and the other had big puffy sleeves. Together with a yellow and black suit, they became my Queen of Hearts.

Queen of Hearts
Original Garment #1

Queen of Hearts
Original Garment #2

Queen of Hearts
Original Garment #3

Making the Costume

1. The skirt of the puffy-sleeved red dress is in two layers. The outer layer goes up to the zipper in the back in ruffles. Cut off the outer skirt and bring it around so the ruffles go up the front. Glue or sew it in place. There is netting between the two layers. Cut the netting up the front and back to the waist, roll it, and glue it in place for side bustles.

2. Cut the skirt of the ruffled red dress off at the waist. Glue the cut edges under. There will be an opening in back where the lower half of the zipper was. Attach half of a shoestring on each side of the opening to close. Remove the red bow from the back to attach to the neck. Glue the skirt from the ruffled dress under the skirt of the puffy-sleeved dress.

3. Cut the blouse of the black and yellow suit into a vest and glue edges under. Pull the vest over the puffy sleeves of the red dress. Split the skirt of the suit open where the zipper is all the way to the hem. Remove zipper. Glue the cut edges of the suit skirt under. Glue the suit skirt to front of the red skirt from the ruffled dress so it will peek through.

4. Put the dress over a hoop skirt.

5. Make a scepter from a dowel rod painted with gold leaf. Cut a red heart from cardboard, cover it with red fabric left over from the ruffled red dress, and decorate with red sequin trim, gold pipe cleaners, and a gold button.

6. For the crown, cover foam with gold fabric and attach two small elastic loops on each side so it can be bobby pinned into the hair.

7. Add long white gloves and a ruffled ruff made from the collar of a man's white shirt, turned backward with stiff ruffles glued on in layers.

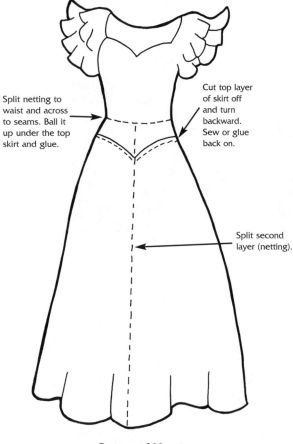

Split netting to waist and across to seams. Ball it up under the top skirt and glue.

Cut top layer of skirt off and turn backward. Sew or glue back on.

Split second layer (netting).

Queen of Hearts
Original Garment #1
Puffy-Sleeved Red Dress

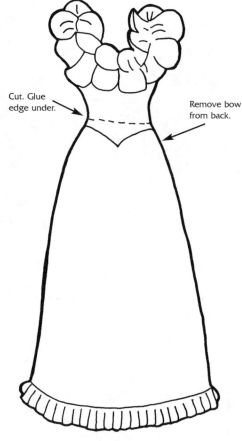

Cut. Glue edge under.

Remove bow from back.

Queen of Hearts
Original Garment #2
Ruffled Red Dress

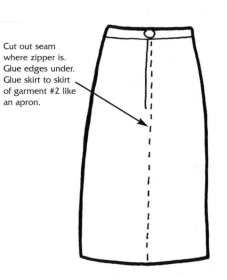

Cut out seam where zipper is. Glue edges under. Glue skirt to skirt of garment #2 like an apron.

Queen of Hearts
Original Garment #3
Black and yellow skirt

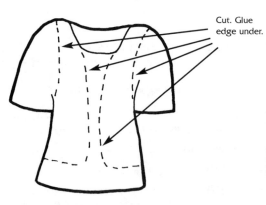

Cut. Glue edge under.

Queen of Hearts
Original Garment #3
Black and yellow top

Gothic Princess

Gothic Princess

In a rummage sale box, I found some rather unusual trim and a belt that snapped closed made of the same trim. It was the perfect enhancement for my Gothic Princess.

Gothic Princess
Original #1

Gothic Princess
Original #2

Making the Costume

1. Dye a light lavender robe and a dark lavender robe with brown dye. They will come out different colors; the light lavender will turn beige and the dark lavender, a dusty rose.

2. Cut a section out of the front of the beige robe from just below the bust to the hem. Glue the edges under. Decorate the belt with black and gold trim and position it below the bust where the robe was cut. Glue the belt at the side seams so it can snap in the back to make it adjustable. Slit both sleeves of the beige robe to the shoulder. Glue the edges under. Glue three pieces of gold trim across the split in each sleeve to hold it together in spots. Glue gold trim and plastic jewels to bodice.

3. Attach a neck ruff. Although you could make a separate ruff, I glued a piece of ruffle inside the neck of the beige robe so that it stood up.

4. Turn the dusty rose robe backward. Glue some of the fabric left over from the beige robe to the bottom. Glue a strip of gold and black trim down the middle from the neck to the hem and the cuffs. Glue white nylon ruffle to the inside of the cuffs. Put the beige robe over top of the dusty rose robe.

5. I cut the brim off a woman's black felt hat, decorated it with the same trim as the robes, a white ruffle, and a scarf to hang down the back.

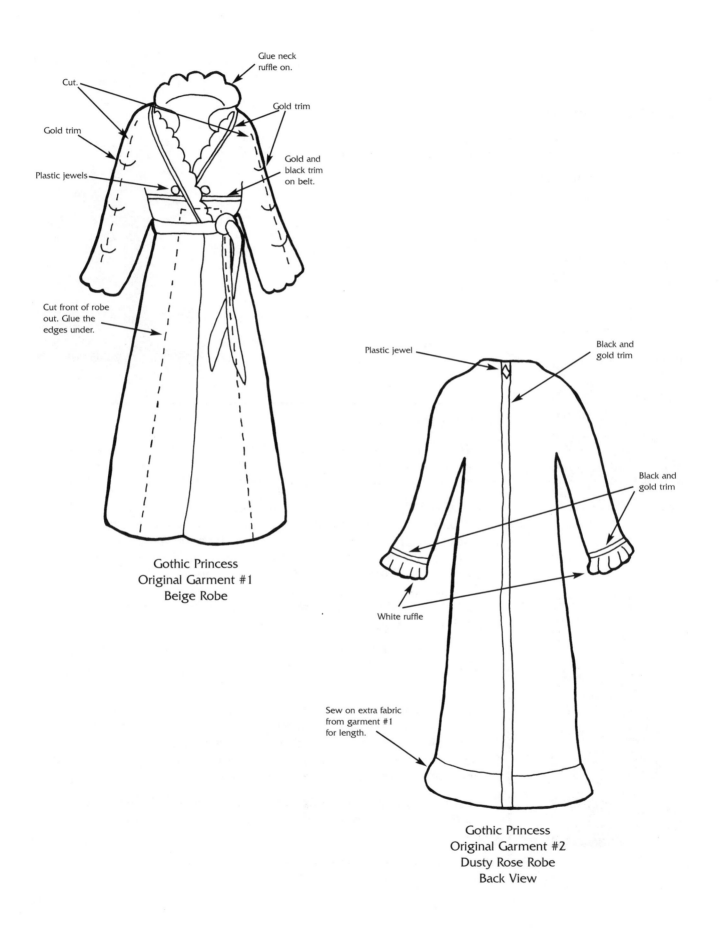

Glue neck
ruffle on.

Cut.

Gold trim

Gold trim

Plastic jewels

Gold and
black trim
on belt.

Cut front of robe
out. Glue the
edges under.

**Gothic Princess
Original Garment #1
Beige Robe**

Plastic jewel

Black and
gold trim

Black and
gold trim

White ruffle

Sew on extra fabric
from garment #1
for length.

**Gothic Princess
Original Garment #2
Dusty Rose Robe
Back View**

Gothic Prince

Making the Costume

1. Dye the pink robe brown. Cut the sleeves out, making the armholes larger for a man. Glue the edges under. Cut the hem to the desired length — around the knee area. Glue the edge under.

2. Cut the white nightgown off to the desired length. Remove the belt from the robe and glue it around the bottom of the nightgown. Split the sleeves of the nightgown up to shoulders. Using fabric leftover from the robe, glue strips of brown "fur" around the splits. Place a full-sleeved white blouse under the white nightgown so the sleeves show through the slits.

3. To make a ruff, cut the collar off the white nightgown, turn it backward, and close with Velcro. Glue on layers of ruffled lace — some up, some down — for that ruff look. Add a wide belt and tights. Put the robe over the top of the nightgown.

4. Make the cape from a red skirt and attach it to the shoulders of the robe with Velcro.

5. The hat is like a large mobcap. Cut two circles out of robe fabric. Glue them together at the edges, wrong side out, leaving a section open to turn the hat through. Turn the hat right side out and the glue the open section closed. Either take tucks with glue to size the hat, leaving a nice brim, or sew in elastic. Glue a feather and broach on. Add a pendant to the neck.

6. I glued strips of robe fabric to men's shoes and made buckles from gold trim to finish the costume.

Gothic Prince

Gothic Prince
Original Garment #1

Gothic Prince
Original Garment #2

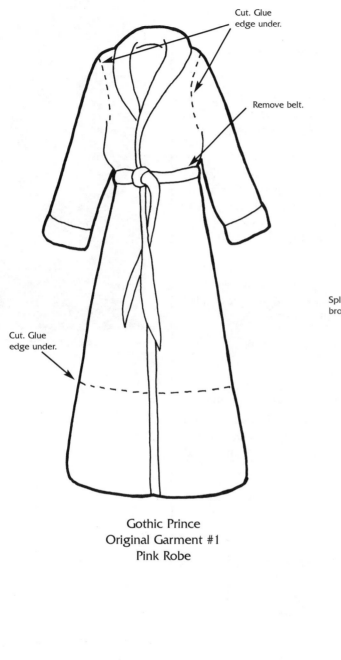

Cut. Glue
edge under.

Remove belt.

Cut. Glue
edge under.

Gothic Prince
Original Garment #1
Pink Robe

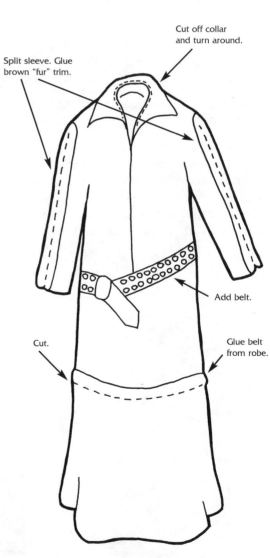

Cut off collar
and turn around.

Split sleeve. Glue
brown "fur" trim.

Add belt.

Cut.

Glue belt
from robe.

Gothic Prince
Original Garment #2
White Nightgown

Cinderella

Cinderella

Over the years, Cinderella has been dressed in different colors and designs, but I chose the original gown done in pale blue with darker blue accents.

Making the Costume

1. Dye a white wedding dress blue by running it through two cycles. The rosettes on the skirt and bodice will dye darker blue.

2. Pull the outer skirt up from the sides to the waist and pin and glue it at the waist to give the skirt that puffy-hipped look. At intervals, pull the skirt up around the edge and glue on rosettes. Add a hoop skirt.

3. Trim the train off to make the hem even with the rest of the dress. Glue the edge under.

4. Add a pearl choker and long white gloves.

Cinderella
Original Garment

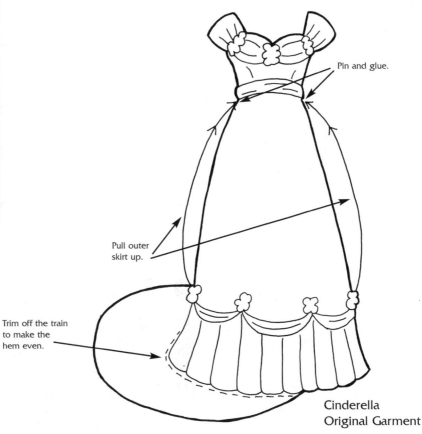

Pin and glue.

Pull outer skirt up.

Trim off the train to make the hem even.

Cinderella
Original Garment

Prince

You can't have a heroine without a prince. He's there to dance with Cinderella, wake Sleeping Beauty and Snow White, even rescue Rapunzel from the tower. He's the ideal man little girls dream of, so he must be well dressed.

Prince

Making the Costume

1. Cut the sleeves of the blue robe out, making the armholes larger for a man. Cut the hem to the desired length.

2. Glue gold trim around the armholes, the hem, and, for decorative purposes, on the front yoke.

3. Add a studded belt. If you can't find one, glue studs onto a plain belt or use fabric paint.

4. Use a skirt for the cape. Attach it to the neck with a piece of white fur cut like a collar and close it with Velcro. I glued a large plastic jewel on each side.

5. Place the robe over a woman's large, ruffled-sleeved blouse.

6. To make sock-like shoes, sew the shoulders of the robe sleeves together, inside out, then turn them right side out and fold them over at the top. Add black tights.

7. Crowns can be made of many things. The prince's crown is coated cardboard covered with fabric and gold leafed. I then glued on fake jewels.

Prince
Original Garment

White fur

Plastic jewel

Red skirt

Gold trim

Cut sleeve out.

Decorated belt

Gold trim

Cut.

T I P

If you can't find men's tights, try women's plus size.

By removing the cape, changing the hat, and adding a ruffled neckpiece and horn made of cardboard attached to a piece of trim, you have **Little Boy Blue.**

Little Boy Blue

Mad Hatter or Romantic Period Man

Robes made of good fabric, such as velvet, make authentic-looking period jackets. I used a dark blue velvet robe in a large size and a purple velour robe to begin my Mad Hatter. The costume can also be used as a man's outfit from the Romantic period.

Mad Hatter or
Romantic Period Man

Making the Costume

1. Remove the belt from the blue robe. Clip off the belt loops. Overlap the front sides of the robe and tack them at desired points using Velcro. Cut the robe short in front with tails in the back. Glue cut edges under. Glue on gold buttons or make gold buttons of fabric paint on the front. Glue on white ruffle trim at the cuffs, leaving a bit showing.

2. Eliminate the ties and close up the purple robe with Velcro the same as you did for the blue robe. Cut the robe off below the waist to make a long vest. (The vest should be long enough to be visible below the jacket you cut from the blue robe.) Cut the armholes larger to accommodate a man. Glue cut edges under. Glue gold buttons on the front or use fabric paint.

3. Put the vest and jacket over a white shirt and blue pants, leaving the collar standing up.

4. Add a white ruffled neckpiece made from a man's white collar. Turn the collar backward, cut out a U, and glue on layers of ruffled trim. Glue a red bow to the center. Add a top hat. For the Mad Hatter, place a card in the hat and add a wig that stands out on the sides.

Mad Hatter or
Romantic Period Man
Original pants and shirt

Mad Hatter or
Romantic Period Man
Original #1

Mad Hatter or
Romantic Period Man
Original #2

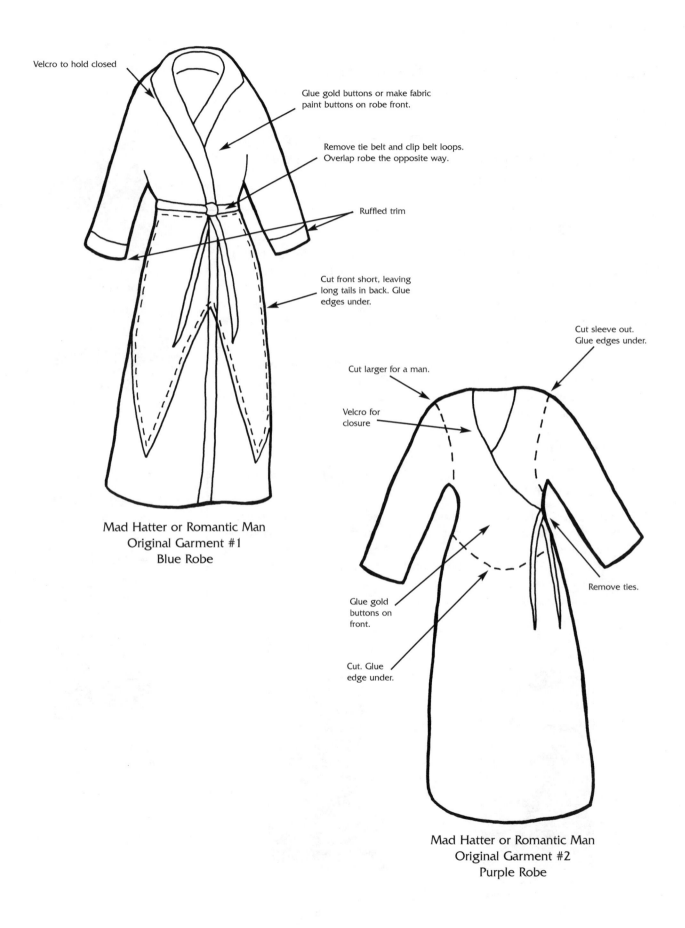

Velcro to hold closed

Glue gold buttons or make fabric paint buttons on robe front.

Remove tie belt and clip belt loops. Overlap robe the opposite way.

Ruffled trim

Cut front short, leaving long tails in back. Glue edges under.

**Mad Hatter or Romantic Man
Original Garment #1
Blue Robe**

Cut sleeve out.
Glue edges under.

Cut larger for a man.

Velcro for closure

Glue gold buttons on front.

Remove ties.

Cut. Glue edge under.

**Mad Hatter or Romantic Man
Original Garment #2
Purple Robe**

Native American Man

I transformed a brown robe, pants, and suede skirt into a Native American Man. Although I usually don't advise dying a dark garment lighter, in this case I needed to bring the color of the robe to a more muted brown. I ran it through two cycles with brown dye to achieve the desired color.

Making the Costume

1. Dye the robe. Cut the top into a vest, rounded in the front. Cut two flaps from the lower sides of the robe and glue them to the tie belt, one in the front and one in the back. Use the remaining robe fabric to make the fringe for the pant legs. Glue it on.

2. The robe sleeves will be used to make leggings. Turn them upside down so the shoulders cover the tops of the feet.

3. Glue fabric from the suede skirt to the shoulders and back of the vest and cut into fringe. Glue fabric to the flaps and cut into fringe.

4. Braid scraps of fabric from an old gold robe, leaving strips hanging down, and glue it to the shoulders and sides of the pants.

5. Add a feathered headband and cuffs made from scraps.

6. The necklace looks real, but it is made of plastic beads and a felt eagle glued on rawhide strips. Add a pair of moccasins, house shoes, or sandals to complete the costume.

Native American Man

Native American Man
Original Skirt

Native American Man
Original Robe

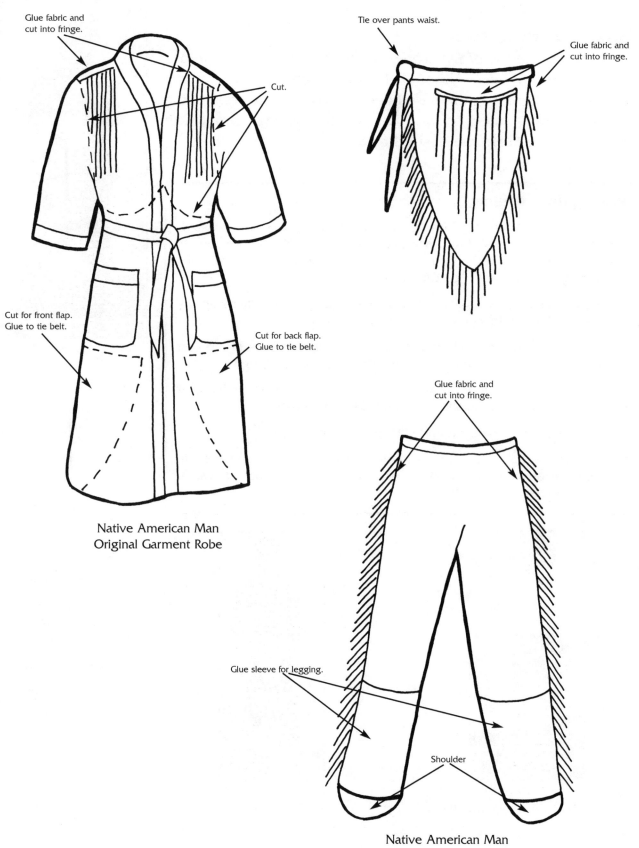

Glue fabric and cut into fringe.

Cut.

Cut for front flap. Glue to tie belt.

Cut for back flap. Glue to tie belt.

Native American Man
Original Garment Robe

Tie over pants waist.

Glue fabric and cut into fringe.

Glue fabric and cut into fringe.

Glue sleeve for legging.

Shoulder

Native American Man
Original Garment Pants

Native American Woman

When you see the robe I started with, you won't believe how this costume turned out. Even I was impressed. I paid fifty cents for the robe at a rummage sale.

Making the Costume

1. Dye the robe brown through three cycles. Cut the black lace away from the bodice.

2. Cut off the cuffs and hem and fringe the edges.

3. With drops of fabric paint, create a beaded look around the yoke, sleeves, and just above the fringe on the hem.

4. Make the belt and headband from the hem you cut off. Decorate them with drops of fabric paint.

5. The necklace is a strand of brown fabric, a concho that slides, and some beads I got from a key ring.

6. Add feathers and shoes.

Native American Woman

Native American Woman
Original Garment

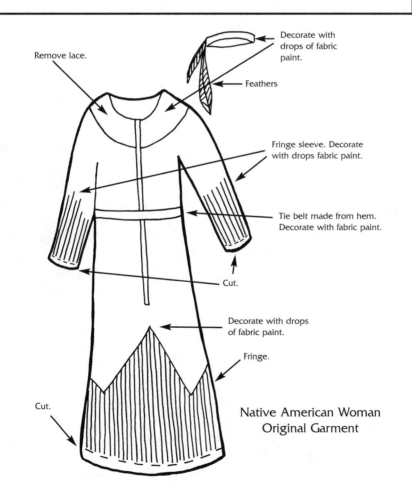

Remove lace.

Decorate with drops of fabric paint.

Feathers

Fringe sleeve. Decorate with drops fabric paint.

Tie belt made from hem. Decorate with fabric paint.

Cut.

Decorate with drops of fabric paint.

Fringe.

Cut.

Native American Woman
Original Garment

Pilgrim Man

Pilgrim Man

Making the Costume

1. Cut the legs of suit pants off at the crotch and discard the waist portion. Cut the inseam out of the pant legs. Press them flat. Glue the edges under. Turn the pant legs upside down so the hems are at the top. Glue the legs together at the corners of the hems. Glue the pant legs to the waist of suit jacket to make it look like a frock coat.

2. Bring the lapels of the jacket together and close with Velcro at the neck. Add a wide belt with a buckle.

3. Cut a pair of pants off just below the knees and glue the edges under. Add long, white socks and shoes with buckles. My buckles were made with cardboard covered with gold trim. Be sure the shoe is a slip-on.

4. Cut the collar and front out of the white shirt down to mid-chest. Cut out the buttons to make two front flaps, but leave the top button intact. Wear the flaps over the jacket, buttoning the collar at the neck.

5. Cut the cuffs off the white shirt. Glue the edges of the cuffs to the inside of the black jacket sleeves. Turn the cuffs out to give the jacket that pilgrim look.

6. Make a buckle to add to a pilgrim-style hat the same way you made the shoe buckles.

Pilgrim Man
Original Garment
Shirt

Pilgrim Man
Original Garment
Suit

TIP To keep the edges of the collar and cuffs from fraying, you can glue them under or glue fabric over them and glue seam binding at the edge, depending on how long you need to use the costume. I did the latter, but I was making the costume for rental.

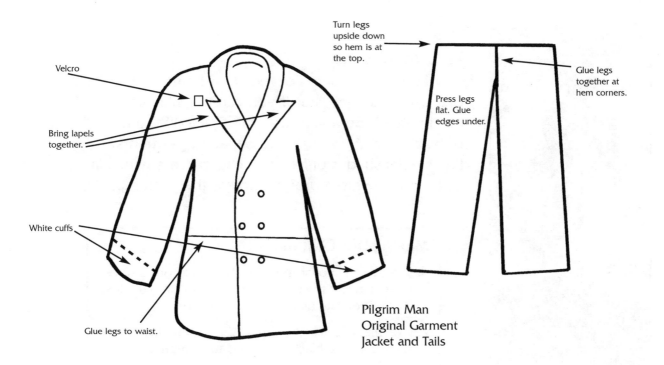

Velcro

Bring lapels
together.

White cuffs

Glue legs to waist.

Turn legs
upside down
so hem is at
the top.

Glue legs
together at
hem corners.

Press legs
flat. Glue
edges under.

Pilgrim Man
Original Garment
Jacket and Tails

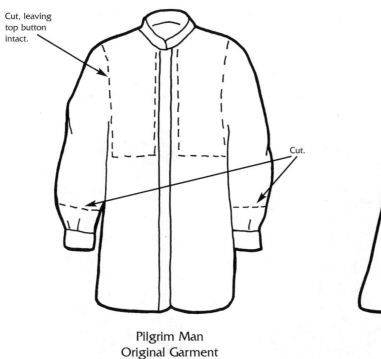

Cut, leaving
top button
intact.

Cut.

Pilgrim Man
Original Garment
Shirt

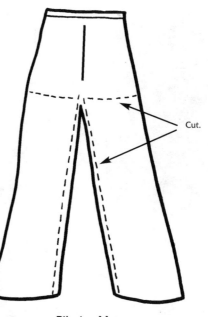

Cut.

Pilgrim Man
Original Garment
Pants

Pilgrim Woman

Pilgrim Woman
Original Black Dress

Pilgrim Woman

Look for a long-sleeved, mid-length, plain black dress. I found one, but if you can't, a skirt and blouse can be used. Be aware that there are different shades of black, and if you use two separate garments, try to find similar shades of fabric. A cheap dress with a large collar and a white apron complete the costume.

Making the Costume

1. Remove the collar from the patterned dress. Press it out flat. Cut the ties off and attach Velcro to close it. Put it on the black dress backward.

2. Use the ties for the cuffs. Glue them inside the sleeves of the black dress and turn them out.

3. Cut the bib off the apron and glue the edge under.

4. The bonnet is constructed on a wedding skullcap. The bill was made from foam (you could use cardboard) and covered with black fabric on the outside and white fabric inside. I cut a circle of white fabric and glued it to the back, like a mobcap, taking tucks wherever needed. Glue a strip of black fabric on where the bonnet meets the brim, leaving long black ties.

5. Add dark hose and shoes.

Pilgrim Woman
Original Collar

Pilgrim Woman
Original Apron

Abraham Lincoln

Lincoln was not only a plainspoken man, but also a pretty plain dresser. He wore a black frock coat, black pants, and a black stovepipe hat. Because I lived in Illinois for many years, I made this costume many times. I couldn't believe my luck when I found a black double-breasted suit with satin lapels. I purchased a second pair of pants and the president was on his way.

Abraham Lincoln

Making the Costume

1. Cut the legs of the black suit off at the crotch and discard the waist portion. Cut the pant legs open at the inseams. Press them out flat. Glue edges under all the way around, except at the hem, which should be intact. Turn the legs upside down so the hems are at the top and glue them together at the corners. Glue the legs around the suit coat under the second set of buttons to make a frock coat.

2. Add the other pair of black pants, a white shirt, and a black tie made of ribbon.

3. The stovepipe hat was one of those cheap foam hats with stripes. It was a bit taller than I wanted, so I tucked it in where the brim meets the hat and glued it in place. Cover the entire hat with black felt and coat with Sculptural Arts Coating.

I used a mask to show you how Mr. Lincoln would look, but this costume can be used for any man from the period. If you have trouble with messy glue that shows on black, keep a Magic Marker handy to cover your mistakes.

Abraham Lincoln
Original Garment

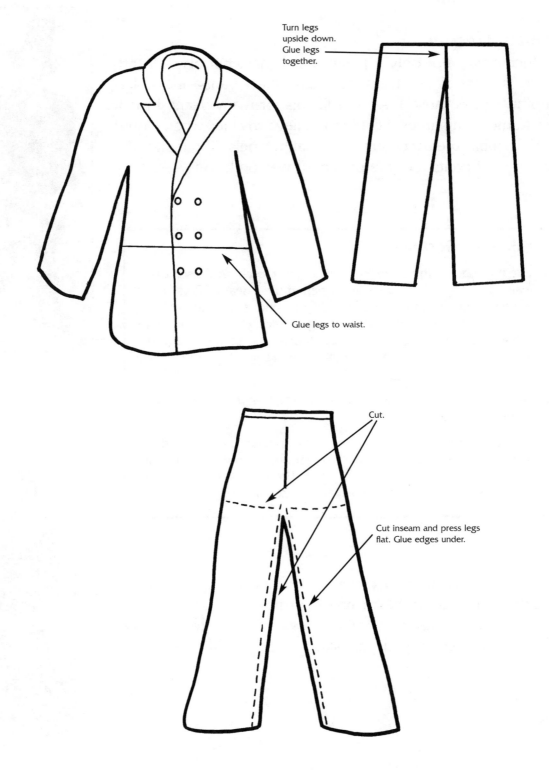

Turn legs
upside down.
Glue legs
together.

Glue legs to waist.

Cut.

Cut inseam and press legs
flat. Glue edges under.

Abraham Lincoln
Original Garment

Mrs. Lincoln

Mrs. Lincoln

You will probably not believe I found a wedding dress rolled up in a box at a rummage sale in Wickenburg, Arizona, for four dollars. I did, and with very little effort, it became a wonderful period dress that might have been worn by the president's wife.

Making the Costume

1. Dye the wedding dress with a bottle of purple dye and three tablespoons of black dye to get that antique look.

2. Let the hem out and press the gown.

3. Cut the train off even with the rest of the gown and glue the edge under.

4. Cut the center out of a black velvet belt that closes in the front with gold balls. Glue the side pieces of the belt together.

5. Gather the raw edges of the train and glue it to the belt to make a short cape.

6. The hat was a man's ball cap. I glued what fabric scraps I had left from the train to the crown of the hat and outer bill. Pull the bill down on the sides so that it sticks up in front and glue the center section of the black velvet belt between the bill and the crown to hold the bill in place. Glue a white lace ruffle to the underside of the bill in layers. Complete the hat with lavender, white, and purple flowers. Add short white gloves.

7. Place the dress over a hoop skirt.

Mrs Lincoln
Original Garment

Glue train to belt
to make a short
cape.

Cut the train off to make the
hem even all the way around.
Glue the edge under.

Mrs. Lincoln
Original Garment

Uncle Sam

I needed an Uncle Sam costume in a hurry, with only a couple of hours until the parade in which he was to appear. What to do? I ran to the thrift store, but could not find a dark blue suit — there was a lighter blue one, though. I grabbed it and hurried on.

A friend said, "Why don't you buy a pair of jams?"

"What's that?" I asked. I'm older, you know. She explained they were like brightly colored cotton sweatpants for summer. Sure enough, I located them in a discount store.

Uncle Sam

Uncle Sam
Original Garment
Jams

Making the Costume

1. Dye the suit a darker blue. Make sure it's a washable suit if you're going to dye it. Cut the jacket off just below the buttons.

2. Cut the suit pants off at the crotch and cut open the inseams. Press the legs out flat to remove the crease.

3. Turn the legs upside down, glue edges under, and glue the hems together at one corner. Round off the bottom edges.

4. Glue the legs to the back of the jacket to form tails.

5. Glue some scraps of red and white fabric from an old dress to the lapels and make cuffs.

6. Glue dark blue sequins around the edges of the jacket, lapels, and cuffs to avoid hemming.

7. Remove elastic from the hem of jams. Press out and glue edges under.

8. Add a navy vest, white shirt and gloves, hat, wig, and beard.

Uncle Sam
Original Garment
Suit

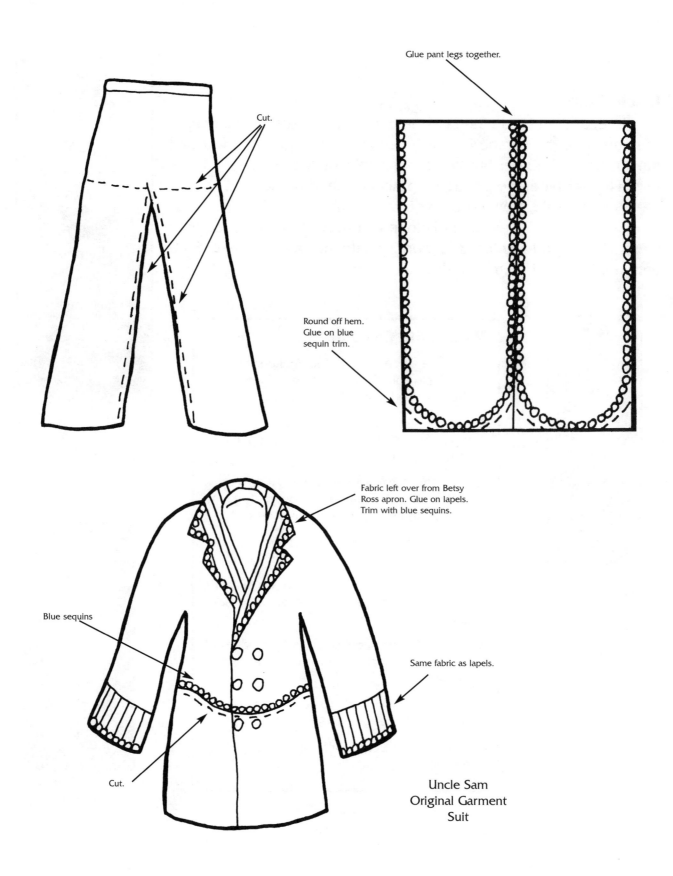

Glue pant legs together.

Cut.

Round off hem.
Glue on blue
sequin trim.

Fabric left over from Betsy
Ross apron. Glue on lapels.
Trim with blue sequins.

Blue sequins

Same fabric as lapels.

Cut.

Uncle Sam
Original Garment
Suit

Mae West

I bought a fabulous hot pink and black dress, but it was short. I needed a long evening gown for Mae West. There was nothing to do but go on the hunt for another dress to add length to it. My good fortune brought me to another pink and black dress. What's the chance of that happening twice? Coupled with an old black dress I already had, I could accomplish my goal.

Mae West

Making the Costume

1. Cut the bottom off the ruffled pink and black dress just above the pink ruffle. Remove the ruffle from the shoulder.

2. Glue or sew the bottom of the ruffled dress to the hem of the big-sleeved dress. Remove the pink rose from the hip of the big-sleeved dress. Glue silver trim across the front and attach a rhinestone broach at the hip.

3. For the train, cut the plain black dress off below the chest. Fold the cut edge into itself twice and glue the waist closed. Glue the skirt to the bottom of the big-sleeved dress, starting under the zipper. Allow it to flow out from the dress. Glue the big pink rose on to cover where you glued the train on.

4. For the headpiece, glue the ruffled sleeve you removed from the ruffled dress to a headband along with pink feathers.

5. Add long gloves, a feather boa, and jewelry.

Mae West
Original Garment #1

Mae West
Original Garment #2

Mae West
Original Garment #3

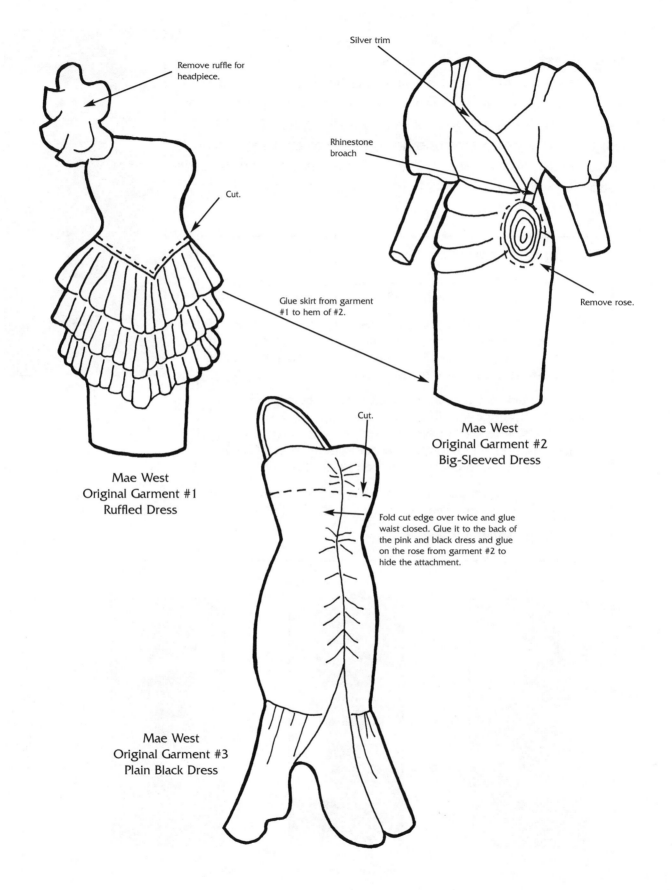

Remove ruffle for headpiece.

Cut.

Silver trim

Rhinestone broach

Remove rose.

Glue skirt from garment #1 to hem of #2.

Cut.

Fold cut edge over twice and glue waist closed. Glue it to the back of the pink and black dress and glue on the rose from garment #2 to hide the attachment.

Mae West
Original Garment #1
Ruffled Dress

Mae West
Original Garment #2
Big-Sleeved Dress

Mae West
Original Garment #3
Plain Black Dress

Ziegfeld Girl

Ziegfeld Girl

Everyone loves a showgirl, and Flo Ziegfeld's were some of the finest. It's hard to believe you can take a dress as pure as a white wedding dress and turn it into a hot showgirl, but it can be done. Follow along.

Making the Costume

1. Dye the wedding dress purple. Cut the outside layer of lace up to the waist and across to the side seams. Trim it so it flows evenly to the back. Cut the sleeves and sheer bodice away from the gown, leaving only the narrow solid sleeve. Pin and glue red sequin trim straps on to hold the dress up.

2. Cut the solid layer of skirting off below the zipper in back, and shorter in front. Glue edge under.

3. Glue a piece of rich purple velvet to the front of the dress. Glue on long gold fringe and red sequin trim to seal the edges and add decoration. To make the tassels for the bodice, double gold fringe twice and glue, then glue them to the upper corners of the bodice.

4. Cut out the original neck and cuffs, cover them with purple velvet, and decorate them with gold fringe and red sequin trim. Attach the edges of the train to the cuffs.

5. The headpiece began as a ball cap with its brim cut off. I glued a chunk of foam to the top, stuck feathers in, and glued them in place. I decorated the headpiece with gold trim, purple netting from the inside of the dress, and a piece of red feather boa. I covered the edges with red sequin trim. Add long gloves and exercises briefs.

Ziegfeld Girl
Original Garment

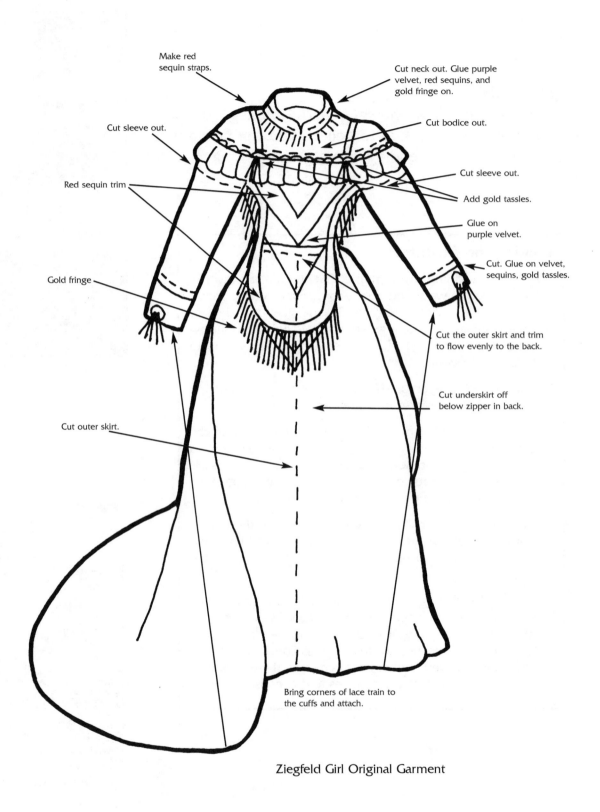

Make red
sequin straps.

Cut neck out. Glue purple
velvet, red sequins, and
gold fringe on.

Cut sleeve out.

Cut bodice out.

Red sequin trim

Cut sleeve out.

Add gold tassles.

Glue on
purple velvet.

Gold fringe

Cut. Glue on velvet,
sequins, gold tassles.

Cut the outer skirt and trim
to flow evenly to the back.

Cut underskirt off
below zipper in back.

Cut outer skirt.

Bring corners of lace train to
the cuffs and attach.

Ziegfeld Girl Original Garment

Calypso Man

As I wandered through a garage sale one sunny afternoon, a bright blue dress caught my attention. The ruffles made me think of the sleeves of a calypso costume.

Calypso Man

Making the Costume

1. Cut the sleeves off the woman's thin black and gold jacket above the elbows.

2. Cut the skirt off the bright blue dress just above the ruffles. Cut out both side seams of the ruffled skirt. Sew or glue a section of the skirt to each sleeve of the jacket. Glue the seams closed. Tie the jacket in a knot in front.

3. The woman's white pants have a drawstring waist and are large enough to fit a man nicely. Roll the legs up and add a colorful sash.

4. Add a straw hat and sandals.

Calypso Man
Original Garment #2

Calypso Man
Original Garment #1

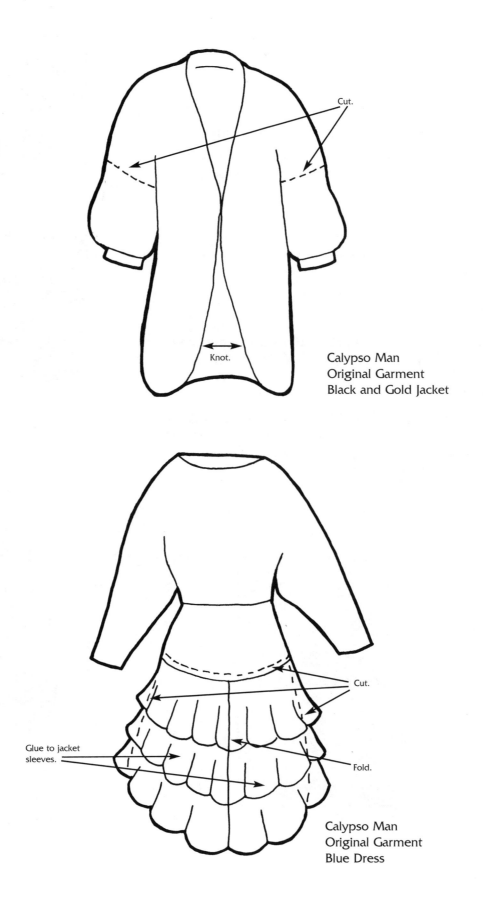

Cut.

Knot.

Calypso Man
Original Garment
Black and Gold Jacket

Cut.

Glue to jacket
sleeves.

Fold.

Calypso Man
Original Garment
Blue Dress

Carmen Miranda

A two-dollar bowl of plastic fruit at a rummage sale inspired my Carmen Miranda. Later, on another excursion into the thrift shop, the dress presented itself to me. The ruffled fabric on the inside and outside of the skirt was taken from an old wedding dress.

Carmen Miranda

Making the Costume

1. Throw the dress and the fabric left over from the trains of wedding dresses into the washer and run through three cycles of orange dye. One train dyed a bit lighter, but I used it on the inside of the skirt.

2. Cut the skirt of the dress off at the hip. Cut the skirt up the side, all the way from the hem through the waist. Use Velcro, snaps, or hooks and eyes to close the waist. Glue bright orange sequins around the waist and to the edges of the skirt.

3. Glue the brighter orange train to the outer skirt so the ruffles hang to the hem and glue orange sequin trim to cover where it is glued on. Do the same with the lighter orange train inside the skirt.

4. Cut the top of the dress off at an angle. Cut off one sleeve. Use hooks and eyes in the back for closure. Decorate and seal the cut edge of the top with orange sequins.

5. Use a man's ball cap with the bill cut off for the headpiece. Glue a chunk of foam on top, glue on fruit to cover, and use orange sequins to fill in the gaps.

6. Add jewelry and exercise briefs.

Carmen Miranda
Original Garment

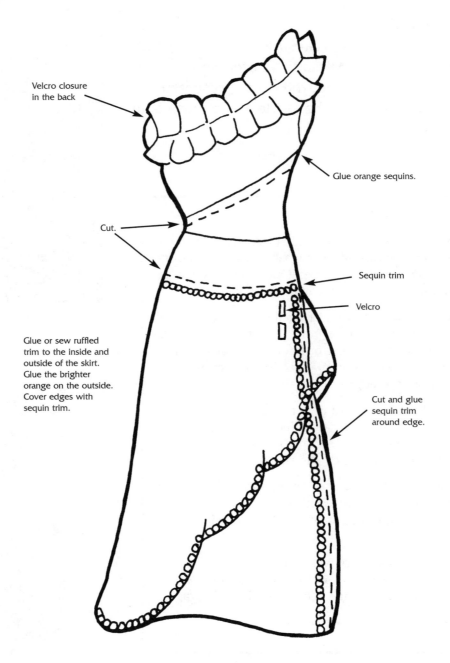

Velcro closure
in the back

Glue orange sequins.

Cut.

Sequin trim

Velcro

Glue or sew ruffled
trim to the inside and
outside of the skirt.
Glue the brighter
orange on the outside.
Cover edges with
sequin trim.

Cut and glue
sequin trim
around edge.

Carmen Miranda
Original Garment

Hansel

Hansel

I could picture Hansel and Gretel walking through the forest on a summer day, hand in hand. He would wear short pants with suspenders, a vest, and one of those little hats that remind me of Peter Pan. She would have a cloth corset over a blouse, skirt, and apron.

I found a three-piece plaid suit for him and pretty much threw her costume together.

Making the Costume

1. Discard the jacket. Dye the pants and vest with one bottle of brown dye through one cycle.

2. Trim the vest off so it's rounded at the bottom and has no buttons or buttonholes. Glue blue sequin trim around the edges and armholes.

3. Cut the pants off just above knees. Glue blue sequin trim around the bottoms, down the sides, and around the waist. Add sequin trim and buttons at front of pants to create a flap look. Add blue suspenders. Glue a piece of fabric left over from the pants between the suspenders and trim with sequins.

4. Put the vest over a woman's large white ruffled blouse; add long white socks and house shoes.

5. The hat is made from two pieces of fabric left over from the pant legs. Glue two rectangles together along the two short sides and one long side, wrong side out. Turn right side out and glue sequin trim to the open edges.

Hansel
Original Garment

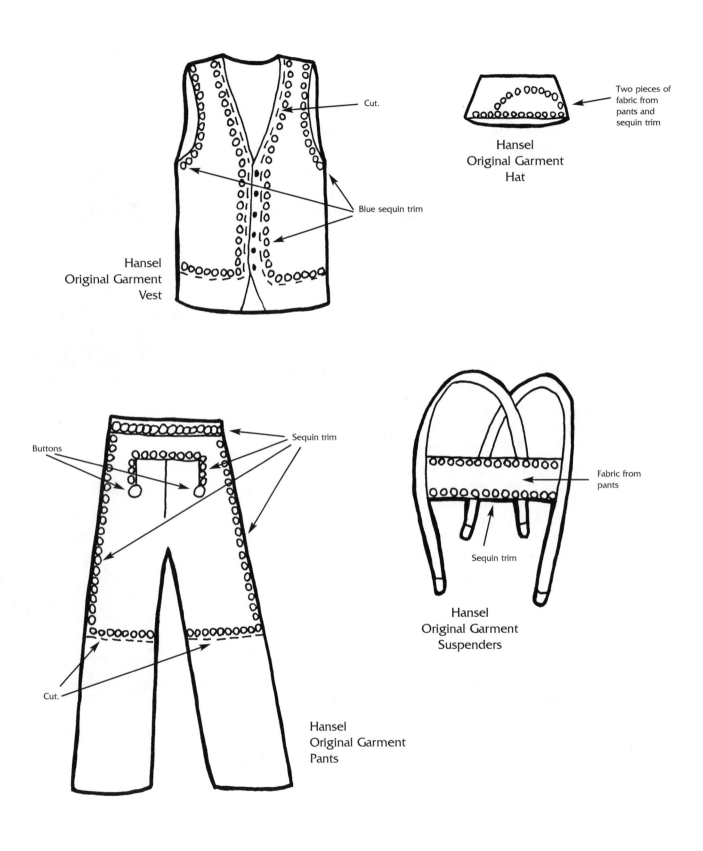

Cut.

Blue sequin trim

Hansel
Original Garment
Vest

Two pieces of
fabric from
pants and
sequin trim

Hansel
Original Garment
Hat

Sequin trim

Buttons

Cut.

Hansel
Original Garment
Pants

Fabric from
pants

Sequin trim

Hansel
Original Garment
Suspenders

Gretel

Gretel

Making the Costume

1. While you're dying Hansel's suit, throw Gretel's red jumpsuit in. Dying it will give it a darker, more muted color.

2. Cut the sleeves out of the jumpsuit. Cut the big collar off and cut out the top of the bodice so the vest will begin just below the chest. Cut the pants off below the waist, leaving the hem in a V. Glue bronze sequin trim to the edges.

3. Remove the bottom buttons, now dyed brown, and glue them on higher up.

4. Glue bronze sequin trim to the hem of the long blouse. Place the vest over the blouse, leaving the tail of the blouse hanging out to act as an apron.

5. Use underskirting under the skirt to hold it out.

6. The headpiece is a visor with silk flowers and ribbons glued on. I added silk flower leis at the wrist and a choker necklace.

Gretel
Original Garment
Jumpsuit

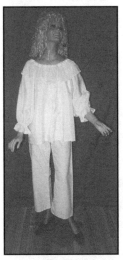

Gretel
Original Garment
Blouse

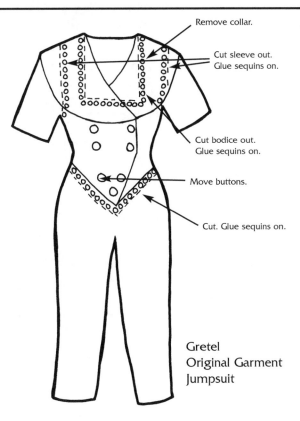

Remove collar.

Cut sleeve out.
Glue sequins on.

Cut bodice out.
Glue sequins on.

Move buttons.

Cut. Glue sequins on.

Gretel
Original Garment
Jumpsuit

Gretel
Original Garment
Skirt

Leprechaun

Leprechaun or Elf

I bought a green jacket at a rummage sale, but there were no matching pants. I ended up dying a pair of white pants green. The jacket and pants aren't exactly the same color, but they're close enough.

By making a few changes to my Leprechaun, he instantly becomes an Elf.

Elf

Making the Costume

1. Dye the white pants green. Cut them off below the knees and glue the edges under. Glue green sequin trim around the bottoms, slightly above the hem, and add a green bow on each side.

2. Glue some glitzy, colorful fabric to the front of a vest of any color and trim with green sequins.

3. Cut the sleeves out of the jacket, leaving a cap sleeve. Cut the jacket at the waist above the second button, leaving it long in the back. Because it is a lined jacket, glue the edges of the lining to the jacket.

4. Cut open the inside seams of the cut-off sleeves and press them out. Trim the sleeves into the shape of tails. Glue the lining to the fabric. Glue the tails to the back of the jacket.

5. Glue green sequin trim wherever needed to cover the edges of the jacket and around the lapels and pocket.

6. Add a white shirt, a bow tie decorated with green sequins, striped socks, and a black plastic top hat or derby with a green feather.

7. The buckles on the shoes are cardboard covered with gold trim. The mask is a Willy Richardson original.

Leprechaun/Elf
Original Garment
Green Jacket

Leprechaun/Elf
Original Garment
Pants

To change the leprechaun into an elf, remove the jacket, make an apron from the back of a leather coat, and add shoestring ties and a neck ruffle. The neck ruffle can be made by cutting the collar and a U out of a man's white shirt, turning it backward so it buttons in the back with the U in the front, and gluing layers of ruffle on the front. The hat is cut from a red and white striped T-shirt and glued together. Add pointed felt shoes, and finish with pointed ear tips if you can find them at your local costume shop.

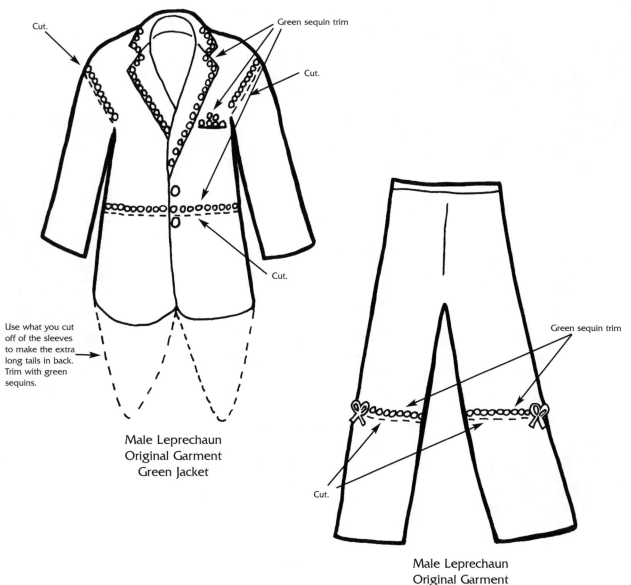

Green sequin trim

Cut.

Cut.

Cut.

Cut.

Use what you cut off of the sleeves to make the extra long tails in back. Trim with green sequins.

Male Leprechaun
Original Garment
Green Jacket

Green sequin trim

Cut.

Male Leprechaun
Original Garment
White Pants

Bo Peep

Bo Peep

I think of Bo Peep in a white ruffled dress with ruffled pantaloons and a bonnet. This is not a difficult costume if you find the right garments to work with. Fortunately, I located the two garments and a large-brimmed straw hat at the same garage sale. The costume was a snap.

Making the Costume

1. Cut the bottom layer of skirt off the dress. Glue the edge under. Glue some stiff lace ruffle trim to the hem of the top skirt.

2. Glue a lace ruffle to the neckline. Cut the hem off the discarded skirting to make a sash. The sash should be long enough to make a bow in back.

3. Glue layers of ruffled trim to the hem of white capri pants up to the knee.

4. Coat the straw hat with Sculptural Arts Coating and let dry. Cut the brim so a wide bill is left in front. Cover the hat with fabric left over from the skirting. Glue ruffled trim under the brim and around the edges. The hat should be worn back on the head so the ruffles under the brim show. Add a sash tied in a bow at the side to hold the hat on.

5. Add white knee-length socks and a crook with a bow.

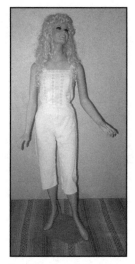

Bo Peep
Original Garment #2

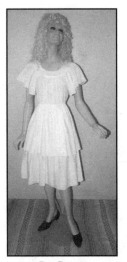

Bo Peep
Original Garment #1

Add ruffle.

Add ruffle.

Cut off.

Cut off for sash.

Bo Peep
Original Garments

Glue on
layers of ruffle
from hem to
below knee.

Bobby Clown

Bobby Clown
Original Garment

Bobby Clown

By removing the clown accessories, the Bobby Clown becomes just an **English Bobby.** This costume is made from a navy suit and an extra pair of pants. It was created for a parade.

Making the Costume

1. Remove the buttons from the jacket of the suit. Bring the lapels together and fasten them together with Velcro. Glue gold braid trim around the collar and cuffs. Sew on the bottom two buttons and glue on the other five above them.

2. Cut one pair of the pants off at the crotch. Cut the inseams out, press the legs flat, and glue the edges under. Turn the legs upside down so the hem will be at the waist. Glue them together at the top at one corner and glue them around the waist of the jacket. Add a belt.

3. The badge is made of thin foam covered with silver and decorated with black fabric paint. It is glued directly to the jacket.

4. On the other pair of pants, glue gold braided trim down the outside of each leg from the pocket to the hem.

5. Add clown accessories and a wig. If you can't find them, check the reference section or the chapters on accessories.

6. I used a Willy Richardson mask rather than a painted face. The mustache is foam covered in doll hair. It can be purchased at most craft shops. The mustache is glued to the mask lip.

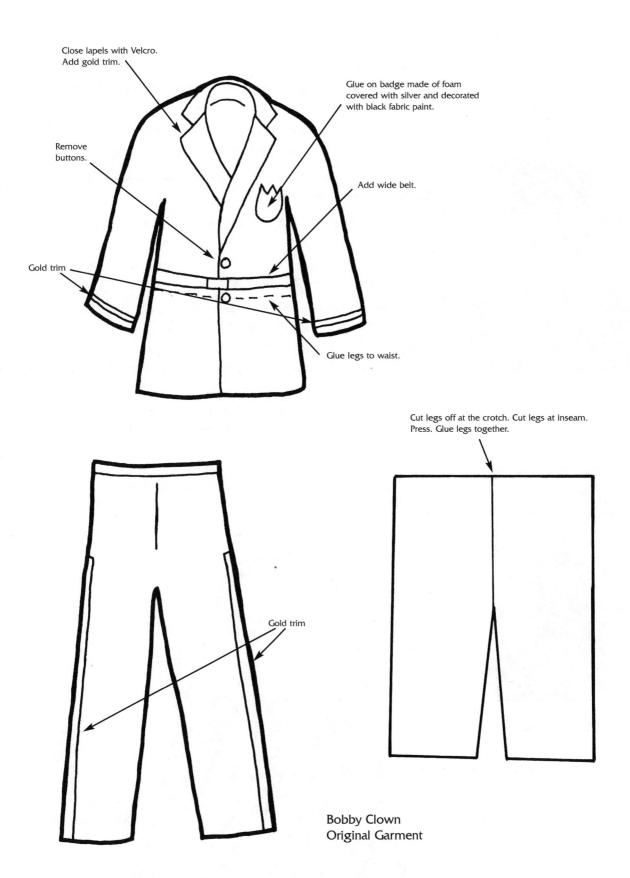

Close lapels with Velcro. Add gold trim.

Glue on badge made of foam covered with silver and decorated with black fabric paint.

Remove buttons.

Add wide belt.

Gold trim

Glue legs to waist.

Cut legs off at the crotch. Cut legs at inseam. Press. Glue legs together.

Gold trim

Bobby Clown
Original Garment

Skirt Clown

Skirt Clown

Clown costumes can be made from many different, everyday garments. I wanted to show you how to take something quite ordinary and transform it into a female clown with very little work. I chose a skirt and blouse.

Making the Costume

1. Cut out armholes in the striped skirt a couple of inches below the elastic waist and glue the edges under.

2. Following the lines of the skirt, glue on colorful sequin trim to give the look of large stems and flowers.

3. Cut some underskirting out of an old prom dress or find a cancan to put under the skirt to help hold it out.

4. The collar is the bottom of a soft white cancan skirt. Because the blouse buttons in the back, I glued the collar directly to the blouse.

5. The oversized mobcap is nothing but a circle of white fabric with the edges glued under or sealed with a ruffle. Attach a strip of elastic or a drawstring a few inches in to give the cap that puffy look.

6. Instead of face paint, I took a plain white plastic mask, glued long eyelashes on it, and decorated it with fabric paint.

7. Add clown accessories.

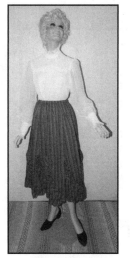

Skirt Clown
Original Garment

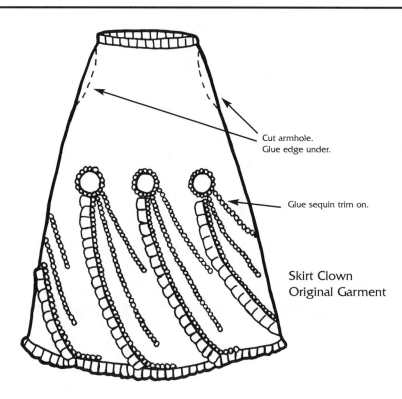

Cut armhole.
Glue edge under.

Glue sequin trim on.

Skirt Clown
Original Garment

Bride of Frankenstein

Picture the Bride of Frankenstein in her flowing white gown, hair standing on end with streaks running up the sides, bolts in her neck and temples, and stitches across her forehead. There's an easy way to achieve the look with very little time, money, and no sewing. The problem is the wig. It can be purchased through the wig house listed in the reference section, but when I made the costume, I had no time to find or order one. *The Simpsons* was popular that year, and the Marge wig would work for what I had in mind. I put it on a wig stand, spray painted it black, and shot some stripes up the sides with white paint.

Bride of Frankenstein

Making the Costume

1. Leaving the zipper up, cut the skirt off the pink and white dress and glue the edge of the top under. Turn backward.

2. Leaving the zipper down, cut the long white skirt off the blue and white dress. Glue edge of the skirt under.

3. Attach the skirt from the blue and white dress to the top of the pink and white dress. Add an inexpensive devil cape, or make a cape from a skirt. Add white gloves.

4. The neckpiece is a black and red garter cut in half with Velcro attached for closure. Glue foam bolts, painted gray, to each side.

5. On a white half mask, paint eyes, make stitches with fabric paint, and glue two more bolts on either side.

Bride of Frankenstein
Original Garment
Pink and White Dress

Bride of Frankenstein
Original Garment
Blue and White Dress

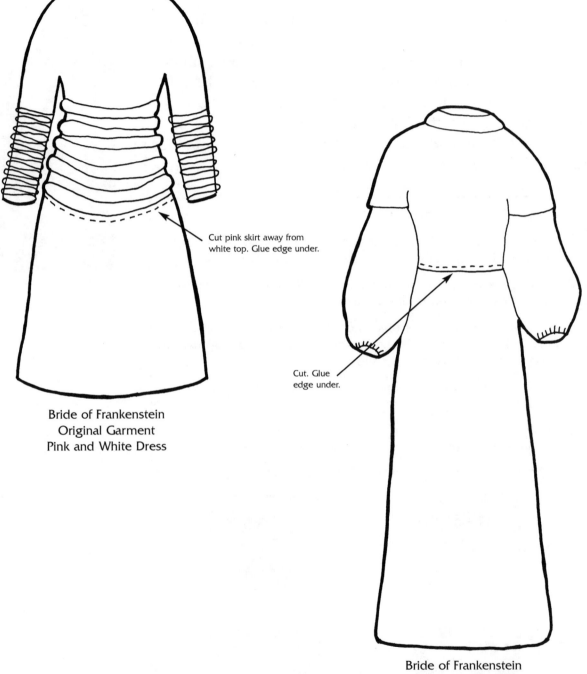

Cut pink skirt away from
white top. Glue edge under.

Bride of Frankenstein
Original Garment
Pink and White Dress

Cut. Glue
edge under.

Bride of Frankenstein
Original Garment
Blue and White Dress

Capes and ponchos are something you must watch for at sales. They make **Rag Coats** that can go with so many costumes. They can be put with almost any horror mask, or even used to make the witch's costume that covers her beautiful gown in *Into the Woods.*

There are a couple of things to keep in mind when making a cape or poncho costume. The main thing is the weight of the fabric. You'll be amazed how much cape and poncho costumes weigh when completed if you don't pay attention. Don't worry about using lighter fabrics that fray. It will only enhance the look. When you wash these costumes, turn them inside out, pin them together, and wash on gentle cycle. Dry the same way on air fluff, or hang to dry.

A **Rag Cape** is the best costume to use up all those old scrap pieces of fabric that aren't really big enough to do much with. The entire costume took me a half hour to make. Lay your cape or poncho out on the floor and start

Cape Hag

gluing the fabric on. Only glue one edge of each piece of fabric to the cape or poncho. When you think it is covered well enough, cut or tear the fabric into strips. How fun is that? Yes, you're done.

Depending on the type of look you're going for, you can add a mask, a hood made the same way, gloves, long fingernails, or a crooked walking stick. You're only limited by your imagination. (See Cape Hag.)

Cape Hag
Original Garment

Chapter 2 Jackets and Pants

The most timesaving, economical idea I ever came up with concerned men's period jackets. In the earlier years of running the shop, I needed men's period coats badly. I couldn't find them, and if I could have, I wouldn't have been able to afford them. One afternoon as I rummaged through a thrift shop, I came across an old double-breasted black suit. That's when the idea hit me.

1800s Jacket

The jacket was perfect at the top. All it needed was more fabric and a flared look from the waist down. It had a pair of matching pants. It might work. I bought the suit for five dollars.

No, it couldn't be that simple. I cut the seams out of the pant legs, pressed the creases out, and turned them upside down so the narrow, hemmed bottoms were at the top. I hemmed around the legs and glued them onto the jacket at the waist. I spot-glued the part of the jacket that hung below the waist to the new flounce I'd made. It was an **1800s Frock Jacket** that could be worn for so many costumes, from Abe Lincoln to the riverboat gambler, depending on what accessories I added. (See 1800s Jacket.)

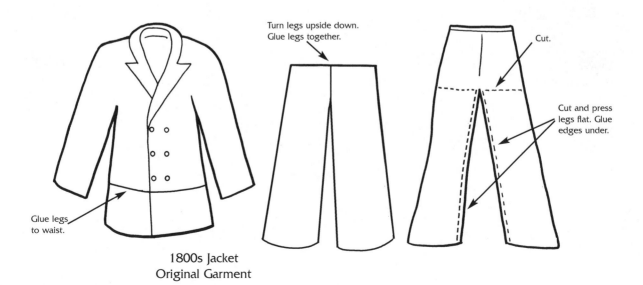

Glue legs to waist.

Turn legs upside down. Glue legs together.

Cut.

Cut and press legs flat. Glue edges under.

1800s Jacket
Original Garment

Civil War
Jacket #1

Excited about my new discovery, I couldn't wait to buy more suits. I wondered, if I found gray and navy blue suits, could I make Civil War soldiers? Yes, yes, yes. You can't imagine what a relief it was to me. I immediately began the hunt for different colored suits. To make the **Civil War Jackets,** I followed the same method, except I brought the lapels to the neck, hooked them with Velcro, glued on gold buttons and gold braiding, and added a gold sash and belt and a pair of gloves. (See Civil War Jackets #1 and #2.)

Civil War
Jacket #2

As I looked at the Union Soldier, it made me think of a **Keystone Cop.** It was simply a matter of changing the buttons, removing the sash, and adding a badge. (See Keystone Cop Jacket.)

When doing a production of *Peter Pan,* I needed a **Captain Hook Jacket.** Again, the costume required a long coat. I used my new method again. To accessorize the jacket like a pirate, I glued strips of red satin from inside the jacket front to the outside, attaching them all the way to the hem. I decorated the jacket with gold trim, gold fabric paint, and black buttons. The cuffs were made by gluing the red satin fabric inside the sleeves and folding it out. I glued the edges together and decorated them. A piece of lace glued inside the cuffs and a sash with a mock belt glued to the front finished the jacket. (See Captain Hook Jacket.)

Keystone Cop
Jacket

Wizard Jacket

I wondered if a woman's suit would work as well. When doing the **Wizard** from *The Wizard of Oz,* I found out. I can tell you, it's not easy to find a man's purple suit. But I found a large-sized suit in the women's clothes. By using the same method I used on the 1800s jacket, my purple Wizard worked. I've found that skirt suits will give you a really full look, too. (See Wizard Jacket.)

Captain Hook
Jacket

British Jacket

Restoration Jacket

Speaking of women's jackets, I found a wonderful red coat to use for a **British Soldier.** It was so simple. I folded and glued the front back to give it that cutaway look and cut the collar off, leaving a small stand-up collar. I glued blue non-fray fabric from the inside of the jacket front to the outside, and did the same with the cuffs. I decorated with strips of gold fabric, gold fabric paint, and gold buttons and glued ruffled lace inside the cuffs. I think Paul Revere would recognize him. (See British Jacket.)

During the Restoration period, men wore tight, fitted knickers and long frock coats. To make a **Restoration Jacket,** I located a woman's gray suede cloth fall coat in a plus size. I folded the collar into itself to give it that small stand-up collar look, removed the buttons from the coat, and cut the hem to the desired length. I folded back the lapels to the hem, showing the blue lining, and glued them back. I glued a strip of gray at the waist to hold the lapels back. I cut off the cuffs and the split the sleeves almost to the shoulders. I trimmed the jacket in blue sequin trim and added gold buttons. Then I added a belt. (See Restoration Jacket.)

| **T** **I** **P** | If you need a loose-fitting, ruffled shirt, look to the women's plus-size blouses. |

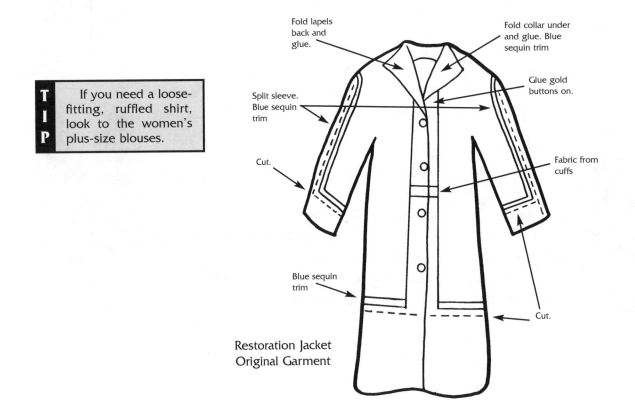

Fold lapels back and glue.

Fold collar under and glue. Blue sequin trim

Split sleeve. Blue sequin trim

Glue gold buttons on.

Cut.

Fabric from cuffs

Blue sequin trim

Cut.

Restoration Jacket
Original Garment

Making a tailcoat from a suit is a bit different. The jacket must be cut off at the waist. Because most jackets are lined, you must then glue the lining to the jacket. If you will be trimming the jacket, the unfinished edges aren't a problem, but if you won't be trimming it, you should glue a hem in before adding the tails. My **Uncle Sam Jacket** was cut off, but not hemmed. I glued the lining to the jacket. Next, I cut the legs off the pants and cut tails from them. I glued sequin trim around the edges. For the red and white striped lapels, I glued fabric from a dress over the lapels and glued sequin trim to the edges. The cuffs were made by gluing a piece of red and white striped fabric inside each cuff and turning it out. Because the piece of fabric was taken from the bottom of the dress, it was already hemmed. I glued the edges of each cuff together and trimmed them. (See Uncle Sam Jacket.)

Uncle Sam Jacket

I'm not sure if the garment I used for the **Blue Velvet Tails Jacket** was actually a velvet robe or a smoking jacket. It seemed too long for a smoking jacket, but too fancy for a robe. It was an elegant blue velvet and long enough to cut tails in without having to use a pair of pants. I cut the front short, tapered the back into tails, and glued the edges under. I removed the existing buttons, closed the jacket with Velcro, and glued on gold buttons. I glued ruffled trim inside the cuffs. (See Blue Velvet Tails Jacket.)

Blue Velvet Tails Jacket

Like the tailcoats, the **Cutaway Jacket** will need to be cut off at the waist. Cut and glue the legs from the pants on as you would for an 1800s jacket. Turn the front edges under and glue them to create the cutaway look. This will give quite a nice period look. Try to find a long-figured vest that hangs below the waist and shows for that period accent. (See Cutaway Jacket.)

Cutaway Jacket

It is easy to find lab coats at thrift shops and garage sales. I buy them a lot. For one thing, they take dye well, so they can be useful in many costumes. Unfortunately, many of them have names embroidered onto the pocket, and unless you can cover the stitching, the coat won't work. When doing *Annie,* I needed a costume for the **East Indian Manservant.** A lab coat filled the bill. I simply put a design over the name and added a colorful sash at the waist. (See Manservant Jacket.)

Manservant Jacket

Elizabethan
Jacket

Pirate King Jacket

Usherette Jacket

Bell Boy Jacket

I love robe fabric and use robes for many costumes. Robe fabric is inexpensive, doesn't fray, and is so versatile. I found a large lady's robe that already had lace around the neck. It was perfect for my **Elizabethan Jacket.** I cut the hem off, split cut the sleeves, and added a belt. I used some of the fabric left over to decorate the sleeves of the black jacket and the bottom of the knickers. (See Elizabethan Jacket.)

My **Pirate King** needed an elaborate-looking, short-sleeved jacket to wear over his puffy-sleeved shirt. I found a large black velvet dress with an elastic waist. I cut the sleeves out, leaving a cap sleeve, cut the hem off, and split the dress down the center front. The finishing touch was to glue gold trim around all the raw edges. I added a red satin sash with a mock belt made of velvet and gold fabric paint. (See Pirate King Jacket.)

Short jackets are made by cutting off suit coats. Glue the lining to the jacket and glue trim around the hem. Leave one button intact at the bottom. I didn't have the gold buttons for my **Usherette,** so I made them from gold fabric paint right on the jacket. After trimming the cuffs and pocket, my jacket was complete. (See Usherette Jacket.)

For the **Bell Boy Jacket,** I chose a navy blue suit jacket. I cut the bottom off, leaving a long point in the front. I cut the collar off and pulled the lapel closed to the neck. Leaving the bottom two existing buttons, I tacked Velcro on from there up to keep the jacket closed. I laid the jacket out flat and glued on gold fabric trim to make it look like a full cover flap in the front. Because I didn't have the buttons required, I covered the existing buttons in gold fabric paint and made the rest of my buttons from the gold paint. I decorated the cuffs and small stand-up collar with gold fabric trim and buttons. (See Bell Boy Jacket.)

Using a woman's black jacket already trimmed in black and white checked lapels and buttons, it was simple to make a **Carhop Jacket.** I cut the bottom off, leaving a point on either side in front. I glued the lining to the jacket and covered the hem with sequin trim. I made a mock pocket on one side and ran sequin trim up the lapels and around the cuffs. (See Carhop Jacket.)

Carhop Jacket

A gold sequin evening coat was the beginning of my **Lady Matador** costume. I cut the coat off above the waist and glued the lining to the jacket. I glued braided gold trim to the hem. I painted some large appliques from a wedding dress with gold leaf and glued them to the neckline, shoulders, and sleeves. I added color with hot pink and red sequin rose appliques on the front and arms. (See Matador Jacket.)

Matador Jacket

Some jackets work just fine the way they are — with a bit of decoration. My **Elton John** costume needed a double-breasted jacket with some glitz. I found a gold woman's jacket and glued on wine-colored sequin trim and large fake rhinestones for the look I wanted. (See Elton John Jacket.)

Elton John Jacket

Going on one of those gambling cruises and they are having a costume party one night? Your costume has to be easy, not too cumbersome, but still interesting. My **Jackpot Jacket** would fill the bill. On a black tux jacket, I designed a slot machine with money falling down the tails and the word *Jackpot* at the shoulders. The entire design was done in fabric paint. The jacket can be worn with slacks and a blouse for the more conservative, or a black leotard and dark hose for those more risky individuals. Add a feathered derby and you're off to the races — or the slot machines. (See Jackpot Jacket.)

Jackpot Jacket

The same method can be used to make a **Rock 'n' Roll Jacket** for a '50s or '60s party. On a white jacket with the tails cut off and hemmed, I used a fabric applique of a jukebox and designed around it with fabric paint and plastic jewels. *Rock and Roll* is painted across the shoulders using drops of fabric paint. So, when everyone else is in poodle skirts (so common) or long white shirts and rolled-up jeans, you will be unique. (See Rock and Roll Jacket.)

Rock and Roll Jacket

Hippie Vest

When you don't have one of those long-fringed hippie jackets, you can make a **Hippie Vest** that will serve just as well. Use any type of vest that hangs below the waist. I glued suede cloth fabric from a second-hand skirt to the bottom and fringed it, then added a strip at the waist and some beads around the waist buttons. (See Hippie Vest.)

Native American Tunic

Native American Tunic

When making a Native American tunic, I was lucky enough to locate a white dress made of a thin suede cloth at a rummage sale. It had long sleeves and a boat neck — very plain, but I knew it would make a wonderful tunic. I purchased a red robe, which would be used for decoration and fringe. For approximately eight dollars, I couldn't believe how beautiful it turned out.

Making the Costume

1. Cut hem off to the desired length.

2. Turn dress inside out; glue an eye-shaped piece of red fabric to both sides of the front. Turn the dress right side out and cut the white fabric away from where you glued the red fabric pieces. Leave enough white fabric around the red fabric to fringe. Fringe around the red fabric.

3. Fringe hem and ends of sleeves.

4. Glue a long piece of red fabric to each sleeve. Fringe.

5. Apply turquoise fabric paint with a brush to the shoulders and part way down the arms. Create a beaded look with drops of fabric paint.

6. Add some long strands of white fabric with bells attached to the shoulders and sleeves. Finish off the tunic with white maribu.

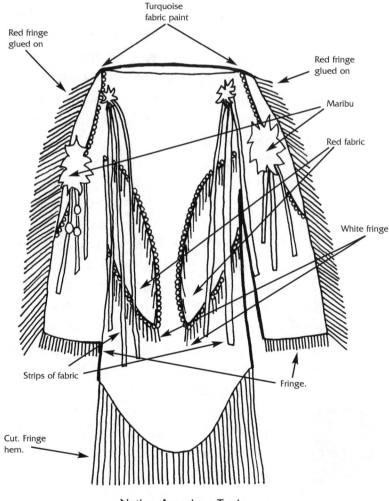

Native American Tunic

Suit pants and a vest are the start you need for a **German Man Costume.** Cut the pants off just above the knee and glue trim around the edge to seal. To give them that flap front look, create a design with sequin trim and gold buttons. The vest is left intact and trimmed with the same trim. Using a piece of fabric from the legs you cut off, glue one side to the middle of the vest. Fasten the other side underneath with Velcro and glue on trim. Add suspenders to the pants whether you need them or not. After all, you are going for a look. (See German Man Costume.)

German Man
Costume

Before zippers, men wore pants that opened on the sides with ties or buttons. When making **Period Pants,** buy women's stretch pants and cut them off to the desired length. If you need a flap look in the front, glue trim and buttons on for an illusion. (See Period Pants.)

Period Pants

To make **Bloomers,** find some wide-legged women's pants that might be worn for a cocktail party or evening wear. A thinner fabric is usually best. Cut a slit in each hem and run a shoestring through each one. Pull the string tight, tie, and you have bloomered pants. (See Sheik Bloomers.)

Some of your storybook characters, Southern belles, and 1800s dresses have **Ruffled Bloomers** underneath. If you find a pair of women's white pants with an elastic waist, you are almost there. Cut them off below the knee and glue layers of ruffles to the legs. To make these full length, don't cut the pants off before you add ruffles to the bottom. (See Ruffled Bloomers.)

Sheik Bloomers

Knickers #1

Shorter **Knickers** that are blousy like the bloomers are made by cutting the bottom of the legs from a pair of elastic-waisted pants and making the openings smaller so they'll fit below the knee. Glue the pants into a band of fabric below the knee, taking tucks to keep that bloomered look. (See Knickers #1 and #2.)

Ruffled Bloomers

If you want to make a man look like a little boy or a character such as **Pinocchio,** use a pair of women's stretch pants that aren't too tight, cut the bottom of the legs off, and glue the hems under. Add the same color suspenders and affix buttons right below them. I glued strips of gold trim down the side of each leg. (See Pinocchio Pants.)

Knickers #2

Pinocchio

Western Chaps

Chaps

Nothing makes a pair of pants look more like cowboy attire than a pair of chaps. Chaps aren't easy to find and they're expensive to buy when you do, so I came up with an easy, inexpensive way to make them. I purchased two brown suede skirts, one darker than the other.

Western Chaps
Original Garment #1

Making the Costume

1. Cut the back out of the lighter skirt, leaving the elastic waist intact. Cut this back section lengthwise so you have two separate pieces.

2. Split the front to the crotch. Glue the pieces from the back onto the bottom of the front to make them look like legs. Round off the legs at the ankles.

3. Use the other skirt for fringe. Glue pieces along the sides and where you glued the leg sections together. Because you'll wear a belt around the waist, the elastic won't show. Make a loop around the back of each leg to hold the chaps against the leg. (See Western Chaps.)

Western Chaps
Original Garment #2

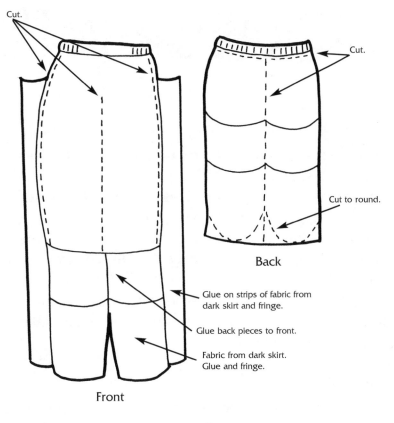

Cut.

Cut.

Cut to round.

Back

Glue on strips of fabric from
dark skirt and fringe.

Glue back pieces to front.

Fabric from dark skirt.
Glue and fringe.

Front

Western Chaps
Original Garments

Fur Chaps normally have to be made. You probably won't find fur skirts to make them. On the sale table at a fabric shop, I found a thin version of lamb's wool in white. I bought two yards of white and a half-yard of black. I laid the pants that would be worn under the chaps on the white fabric and cut around them, leaving several extra inches around the sides. I made the waist with a two strips of white glued together with Velcro in the back for closure. I cut a V out of the front of the leg piece and glued the legs to the waist. Then I cut out odd shapes of black fabric and glued them on for that cow-like look. Add a loop in back behind each knee to hold the chaps against the leg. (See Fur Chaps.)

Fur Chaps

Chapter 3 Costumes for Children

Throughout my costuming career, I did not do many children's costumes, except by special order. This was mainly because it was more difficult to find second-hand clothing that worked well for smaller sizes. Today, it seems children are getting larger and adults are getting smaller. The stores have begun carrying women's sizes beginning at 0. Therefore, I can find adult sizes small enough to fit children without much conversion.

This is the one chapter in the book that includes patterns that involve any real sewing, and it is mostly taking tucks and straight-line sewing.

Child Princess

The first dress I located to make my Child Princess costume was a size 3. It was so small I couldn't get the zipper up on the back of my mannequin. It was a deep red velvet with pink satin peeking through the sleeves and bodice and an empire waist.

Child Princess

Making the Costume

1. Starting in the center, just below the empire waist, cut the skirt open and taper it to the back. Cut the hem off.

2. Glue sequin trim to the raw edges where you cut, leaving the front open.

3. Decorate the bodice, sleeves, and neck with sequin trim.

4. Add a sequin belt that ties in the back.

5. I added a pink skirt with elastic waist to show in the front and a tiara made of pipe cleaners and sequin trim.

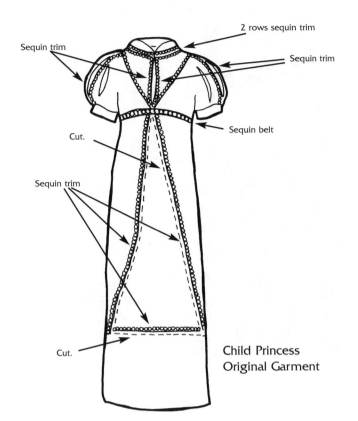

2 rows sequin trim

Sequin trim

Sequin trim

Sequin belt

Cut.

Sequin trim

Cut.

Child Princess
Original Garment

Child Princess
Original Garment

Making a **Flapper Costume** for a child is simply a matter of finding a skirt with an elastic waist. Pull the waist up above the child's chest, add straps, and glue fringe and sequins on. Don't glue sequin trim all the way around the top because if you do, the elastic will no longer stretch. Just add sequins to the front. I glued on hot pink maribu trim to cover the straps. The hat was a woman's felt hat, pulled low with two flowers and feathers glued to one side. The choker is stretch sequin, and the beads are Christmas beads. The costume still needed something, so I cut the arms out of a black stretch leotard, glued the upper edge under, used them as long gloves, and the outfit was complete — and very easy.

Child Flapper

Child Flapper
Original Garment

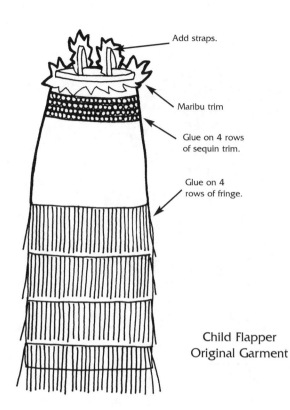

Add straps.

Maribu trim

Glue on 4 rows
of sequin trim.

Glue on 4
rows of fringe.

Child Flapper
Original Garment

Native American Child

Native American Child

You will have to do one line of sewing for the Native American Child. I found a long tan woman's robe with long sleeves to start.

Making the Costume

1. Dye the robe brown. Cut the front center panel out on both sides. Glue or sew the sides back.

2. Cut the hem and sleeves off, leaving enough fabric to fringe.

3. Glue pieces of the fabric cut from the bottom to the bodice and the backs of the sleeves. Cut into fringe.

4. Add any trim desired and do beading with drops of fabric paint.

5. Make a headband of the same fabric, creating a beaded look with drops of fabric paint. Use a tie or Velcro to hold the headband on.

Native American Child
Original Garment

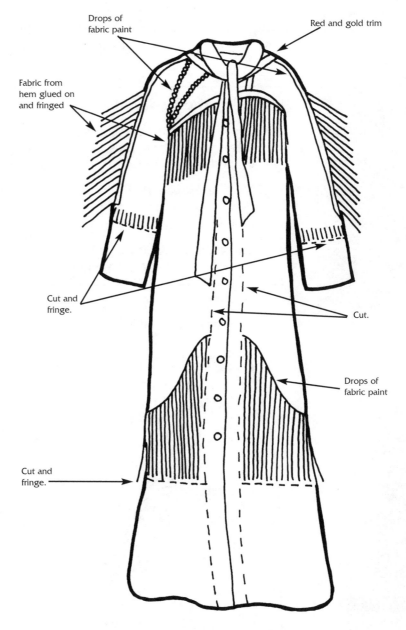

Drops of
fabric paint

Red and gold trim

Fabric from
hem glued on
and fringed

Cut and
fringe.

Cut.

Drops of
fabric paint

Cut and
fringe.

Native American Child
Original Garment

Child Movie Star

Child Movie Star

Every little girl loves the idea of being a movie star. Making a movie star costume is a matter of finding a long glitzy gown and feather boa. I started with a pair of purple velvet pants.

Making the Costume

1. Convert the elastic-waisted pants into a dress by cutting the inseams out of the legs. Sew the legs together straight down on both front and back and clip the crotch out.

2. Glue appliques to the front of the dress. Glue a string of rhinestones to a flat shoestring to attach to the bodice and go around the neck.

3. Cut the sleeves off the shirt and glue the edges under to use as long gloves. Add a feather boa.

Child Movie Star
Original Garment

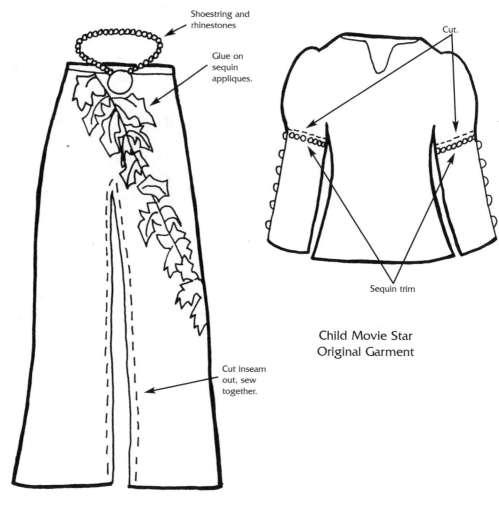

Child Movie Star
Original Garment

Child 1800s Gown

An off-white lined cotton dress with long sleeves decorated in flowers and ribbon was the beginning of my child's 1800s gown.

Making the Costume

1. Take tucks on either side of the back zipper.

2. Add four rows of pink loop trim to the bodice.

3. From waist, split the outer skirt, tapering it to the back. Cut the skirt lining off longer and trim both layers of skirt with lace and pink loop trim. Cut the sleeves off at the wrists and decorate the edges with pink loop braiding.

4. Add a woman's long nightdress underneath to hang below both skirts. See bonnets in the Hats and Headpieces section for how to create the hat.

Child 1800s Gown

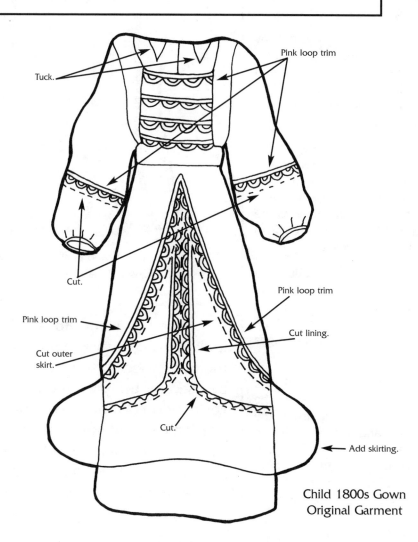

Tuck.

Pink loop trim

Cut.

Pink loop trim

Cut outer skirt.

Pink loop trim

Cut lining.

Cut.

Add skirting.

Child 1800s Gown
Original Garment

Child 1800s Gown
Original Garment

Medieval Child

Medieval Child
Original Garment

Medieval Child Costume

For a medieval costume, you'll want a dark, heavy fabric. I found a dark burgundy cocktail dress that zips up the back and a black velvet skirt.

Making the Costume

1. Take a tuck on either side of the zipper in the back of the cocktail dress. Bring the low-cut neckline right up to under the chin.

2. Cut the bottom off the black velvet skirt and glue it to the hem of the cocktail dress.

3. Split the skirt from the hem to below the knee and glue sequin trim onto the raw edges.

4. Decorate the costume by gluing dark sequin trim, gold sequin trim, and appliques where desired. Add pink fringe to the bodice.

5. To make the cape, cut the back out of what remains of the black velvet skirt. Glue trim around the edges and attach the skirt piece to the shoulders of the cocktail dress with Velcro.

6. Cut the sleeves out of a woman's black leotard and cut the wrists to form a point at the hands. Glue sequin trim along the edges of the point.

7. Cut the bill off a ball cap, cover the crown with the remaining fabric from the skirt and decorate it to match the rest of the costume. Add a gold necklace.

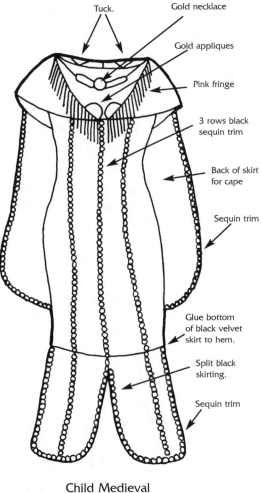

Child Medieval
Original Garment

When making **Boys' Costumes**, look through this book. The same methods used for men's costumes can be used for the younger men's clothes. For period costumes, you may have to use female clothing. Remember, if you must use an adult-sized hat for a child, glue a strip of foam on the inside that is the width you need for that perfect fit.

Child Teddy Bears

What can you do with a teddy bear? Make a costume, of course. I had three small children as customers whose mother wanted them to be the Three Bears. Small children do not like to have their faces covered. They'll wear a hat, gloves, even house shoes, but don't cover their face.

My costumes were constructed from three children's ball caps and three teddy bears.

Making the Costume

1. Cut the bills off three ball caps with adjustable backs.

2. Cut the heads off three teddy bears.

3. Leaving most of the stuffing in, glue the heads to the ball caps. Leave a loose edge in back where the ball cap adjusts. Glue the head down above the adjustment and leave some fur hanging over it.

4. Decorate the bears. Baby Bear needed no decoration; Papa Bear got a straw hat; and Mama Bear got glasses and a mobcap.

5. Cut the front paws off the teddy bears, remove stuffing, and glue the paws onto gloves.

6. Cut the feet off the teddy bears, remove stuffing, and glue to house shoes.

7. Add appropriate clothing found in thrift shops.

Child Papa Bear

Child Mama Bear

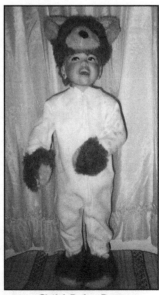

Child Baby Bear

Section II
Accessories

Chapter 4 # Hats and Headpieces

In my opinion, headwear is one of the most important accessories. Throughout the centuries, headwear has told us so much about the wearer. When headwear was prevalent, the observer knew certain things at a glance: what social class the individual belonged to, whether the person was conservative or flamboyant, if he was a member of the military, and if so, what rank.

Although hats are still worn for special occasions, such as weddings and funerals, or for utilitarian purposes, such as keeping the harmful rays of the sun from our faces, for the most part, we are not a hat-wearing society. Many of the hats and headpieces needed for productions, parades, or masquerades can only be found in antique shops — and the prices — wow!

Of course, hats can be purchased from specialty houses and costume shops, but again, the prices for something really nice can be high. What I've attempted to do in this chapter is to show you how to make the desired headwear from easy-to-find products that don't cost an arm and a leg.

We will be using all manner of straw hats, felt hats, ball caps, even the bottom of plastic bottles to create the illusion of period hats, glitzy showgirl headpieces, and hats for productions, parades, and masquerades. If the products used for each project are not easily accessible, look to the reference section for where to buy them. Remember, headwear can make or break even the best costume.

Straw

The straw hats everyone seems to buy on vacation usually end up stuck in a closet or the garage; occasionally they are decorated and hung on a wall. Eventually, they are tossed in the bag for a thrift store or show up in a rummage sale.

Straw hats come in all shapes and sizes, sometimes colors, and they are a cheap, versatile product to use in costuming. One of the problems of working with straw is that it comes apart when it is cut. When it is bent, it tends to break in the area of the bend after a while. Painting it can also cause problems. Most paints will make straw hats stiff, and the paint tends to crack and peel when the hat is bent. And after it's painted there is still the problem of cutting the straw without it coming apart. What to do?

I have solved these problems with a product called Sculptural Arts Coating. (See reference section for where to purchase.) Sculptural Arts Coating is a white, paste-like product that dries clear and stays flexible. It gives wonderful texture and body to the straw, and, once applied, you can bend, cut, glue, and decorate the hat.

If you wish to have a different color of straw, merely add some dry dye to the Sculptural Arts Coating and stir it in well. The coating will dry a darker color than the mix. For example, if you add black dye, the coating will appear gray when wet, but it will dry black. If you have an odd-colored gown or dress and wish to make a hat to match, apply a coat of Sculptural Arts Coating, press fabric from the dress into it, and apply another coat over the top. Remember, the coating dries clear, so the color of the fabric will show through.

We will begin with hats made from a ladies' large-brimmed straw hat. If you want an 1800s style, there are several ways to go.

Ladies' Large-Brimmed Straw Hat #1

Making the Hat

1. Leaving the hat the natural straw color, apply a coat of Sculptural Arts Coating and let dry.

2. Bend the back of the brim up to the crown and glue.

3. Decorate the hat with feathers and flowers.

Large Brim Straw Hat #1

Ladies' Large-Brimmed Straw Hat #2

Making the Hat

1. This hat was done to match a dress. Leave the brim as is. Apply a coat of Sculptural Arts Coating. While wet, press fabric from the dress onto it and apply another coat on top of the fabric.

2. Do the same thing with strips of fabric on the underside of the brim. Let dry.

3. Trim the edges by gluing a complementary color of sequin trim to the edge of the brim and around the crown.

4. Decorate the hat with feathers and flowers.

Large Brim Straw Hat #2

Ladies' Large-Brimmed Straw Hat #3

Making the Hat

1. Sprinkle one teaspoon of purple dye into a cup of Sculptural Arts Coating. Keep stirring until well mixed. Apply coating to the underside of the brim first, then set the hat on a styrofoam head and cover the top with an even coat. Let dry.

2. Add some fabric for a design and trim around the edges with sequins.

3. Add feathers and flowers, leaving some feathers hanging over the edge of the brim.

Large Brim Straw Hat #3

Ladies' Large-Brimmed Straw Hat #4

Large Brim Straw Hat #4

Making the Hat

1. This hat is orange. Add a coat of Sculptural Arts Coating and let dry.

2. Bring up the back of the brim off to one side and glue to the crown.

3. Add an orange ribbon and white trim around the crown.

4. Decorate with flowers and feathers and a big bow from a wreath.

Ladies' Large-Brimmed Straw Hat #5

Large Brim Straw Hat #5

Making the Hat

1. Apply a coat of Sculptural Arts Coating. While the coating is still wet, press white wedding fabric into it and add another coat. Let dry.

2. Lay the neckline of a sheer white cape overlay with rhinestone trim against the crown. Glue the rhinestone edge to the edge of the brim and spot glue it to the hat, leaving material hanging down the back.

3. Decorate with white feathers and flowers.

4. Wrap the material hanging down the back around the neck for an elegant look.

Another use of large-brim straw hats is for bonnets. Because we're using the Sculptural Arts Coating, the brim can be cut away from the crown and glued on in a different way.

Bonnet #1

Making the Hat

1. Apply a coat of Sculptural Arts Coating. Let dry.

2. Cut the brim away from the crown.

3. Cut a section of the brim into a heart shape along the outer curve.

4. Glue the heart-shaped section of the brim to the crown so it stands up.

5. Cover the brim section with fabric by gluing the fabric to the edges. Glue on trim to cover where the fabric is glued on.

6. Glue on a sash where the brim and crown are connected. Leave the sash long enough to tie under the chin.

7. Decorate with flowers.

Bonnet #1

Bonnet #2

Making the Hat

1. Apply a coat of Sculptural Arts Coating. Let dry.

2. Cut the brim away from the crown. Cut a piece of the brim into a large half-moon.

3. Glue the brim piece to the crown. Glue a white mobcap to the crown.

4. Glue layers of white ruffle on both sides of brim.

Bonnet #2

Bonnet #3

Making the Hat

1. Apply a coat of Sculptural Arts Coating.

2. While the hat is still wet, press fabric onto the crown only. Add another coat over the fabric. Let dry.

3. Cut the brim away from the back, leaving the front intact.

4. Glue on fabric to both the top and bottom of the brim, starting at the crown and working out to the edge of the brim. Tuck fabric along the way.

5. Glue on ruffle trim at the edge of the brim.

6. Glue a sash on where the brim and crown meet, leaving enough to tie under the chin.

7. Decorate with flowers.

Bonnet #3

Bonnet #4

Bonnet #4

Making the Hat

1. Sprinkle a teaspoon of dry, dark brown dye into a cup of Sculptural Arts Coating. Mix well. Coat the straw hat evenly and let dry. Be sure you coat underneath the brim.

2. Cut the brim away in the back, tapering to the front.

3. Glue on a tie where the brim and crown meet, leaving enough to tie under the chin.

4. Glue a double ruffle on both the top and bottom edges of the brim.

5. Glue a bow on the top of the brim.

If you happen to come across a smaller-brimmed straw hat and are in need of a 1900s hat, try the following pattern.

Miss Kitty

Miss Kitty

Making the Hat

1. Apply a coat of Sculptural Arts Coating. Let dry.

2. Bring both sides of the brim up to the crown and glue.

3. Glue some brown velvet to each side to add color.

4. Glue on trim to cover where velvet is glued on.

5. Add a large, dark brown flower to the front.

6. Glue on yellow flowers, yellow feathers, and red feathers for accents.

What do you do for smaller hats? Very simply, you don't use the brim — but save it because you may need it for something else later. Because we'll be coating the crown anyway, you might as well coat the brim, too. That way if you need a brim for another project, it's already prepared.

Twenties Hat #1

Twenties Hat #1

Making the Hat

1. Apply a coat of Sculptural Arts Coating. Let dry.

2. Cut the brim away from the crown.

3. Glue hanging beads around the back and sides.

4. Glue on sequin appliques to cover the hat.

5. Glue beads around the edge of the crown. Glue on a large flower and two feathers.

If you want a **Simpler Twenties Hat,** coat your straw hat and cut the brim off. Glue stringed sequins around the crown until it is covered. Glue a feather and flower to one side. (See Twenties Hat #2.)

Twenties Hat #2

Another use for the crown of a straw hat is for **Harem Headpieces.** If the crown is too large, coat it and let it dry, then cut it to the size you desire. The harem headpieces can range from plain to fancy depending on the trim used. Be sure you glue the edges of your face scarf onto the hat before gluing on the trim. That way, the trim will cover the scarf edges. (See Harem Headpieces #1 – #3.)

Some crowns are taller and more squared instead of rounded. Once these crowns are coated and dry, they can be used to make a very nice hat for a man.

T I P   If the straw hat is too large or slips around, glue a strip of foam inside near the edge.

Harem Headpiece #1

Harem Headpiece #2

Harem Headpiece #3

Fez

Fez

Making the Hat

1. After coating the hat, add red fabric, first to the top, then around the crown. Add another coat of Sculptural Arts Coating and let dry.

2. Trim the edges with gold sequins.

3. Glue a tassel to the top and glue a gold button over it.

Turban

Pith Helmet #1

Pith Helmet #2

Men's Gangster

Men's Bowler

Men's Gambler

If you happen to need a **Turban,** follow the instructions for the Fez. Next, fill the sleeve from a lightweight jacket with fiberfill, twist some gold sequins around it, and glue it to the Fez. Add a feather and decoration in front. It made an easy, wonderful turban. (See Turban.)

For men, you will find straw hats in the shape of **Gangster Hats, Bowlers,** even **Gamblers** from the 1800s. Because there is no cutting or decorating to speak of, making a hat out of these is simply a matter of adding dye to Sculptural Arts Coating and coloring the hat.

Another example of a man's hat that's difficult to find but easy to make from a straw hat is the **Pith Helmet.** By coating the hat and pressing on strips of beige fabric, you can achieve the look quite easily. Add a leather strap and you're ready for any safari. For the women's counterpart, add white sheer fabric around the crown, allowing it to hang down the back. (See Pith Helmets #1 and #2.)

TIP
Be sure you do not use too much dry dye in your mix or it will ball up and look terrible. You just need enough to achieve the desired color. It will dry darker than it looks when it's wet. You may have to use more than one coat with light colors.

Chinese Hat

Chinese hats are normally made of straw, but I located one that was made of styrofoam. It was very lightweight and had a string tie. It was quite inexpensive. Of course, the problem with styrofoam is that it breaks easily. I found the solution for that.

Chinese Hat

Making the Costume

1. Coat the inside of the hat with Sculptural Arts Coating. Let dry.

2. Coat the outside with Sculptural Arts Coating. While wet, press a piece of thin red fabric into it and let dry.

3. Glue gold trim around the edge.

4. Glue a black feather boa to the crown and allow it to hang down the back for a pigtail look.

Ball Caps

When making headpieces, especially the more unusual pieces, I've found men's ball caps to be a great base. Stay away from the mesh caps or ones with plastic. The glue will adhere to fabric and hold much better. With the bill removed and the adjustable back intact, these caps are a perfect beginning.

For the first example, I found some balsa wood fruit at a rummage sale. I glued sequins on each piece of fruit for a glitzy look. If you don't have sequins, you could use glitter paint.

Glitzy Fruit Headpiece

Making the Hat

1. Remove bill from ball cap.

2. Glue gold lamé fabric around lower portion of the hat, leaving the adjustment in back unglued.

3. Glue a big satin bow to back.

4. Glue gold Christmas beads from sides to back, letting them hang down.

5. Glue sequined fruit to top of cap.

6. Glue black feathers to back and a sequin applique over the stems where they're glued.

7. Trim with sequins and gold beads.

Glitzy Fruit Headpiece

If you're looking for a more **Natural-Looking Fruit Headpiece,** glue artificial plastic fruit to a ball cap, placing the grapes around the edges to cover the cap. If you have empty spaces, simply glue in silk leaves or green sequins. (See Natural Fruit Headpiece.)

Natural Fruit
Headpiece

Ball Cap Showgirl

Ball Cap Showgirl

Showgirl headpieces can be done easily with the ball cap base. Remember, if you are going to have hanging beads, glue them on first so you can cover up where they're glued on. If the headpiece is going to be too heavy and you need an elastic chinstrap to hold it on, use a safety pin to secure the strap on each side. Glue a piece of felt or foam on the inside where the pin shows. The part of the pin showing on the outside will be covered by whatever you use for decoration.

Making the Hat

1. Remove the bill from a ball cap.

2. Glue hanging beads to the edge of the cap. I used beads from a beaded curtain.

3. Glue a piece of cardboard cut to match the shape of black and silver sequin appliques to the top of the cap so it stands up. Glue appliques to both sides.

4. Cover the cap with black, silver, and royal blue sequin appliques.

5. Glue white feathers behind the stand-up appliques.

There was an occasion when I was asked to design a **Lion King** costume for a children's production. I started with a ball cap, removed the bill, and pinned on an elastic chinstrap with safety pins. I pinched the heads of the safety pins so they could not come undone and covered the pins with a piece of foam on the inside of the cap.

Lion King

The easiest way to cut the yarn is to find a piece of cardboard or plastic, wrap the yarn around and around it until you have a sufficient amount, and cut both ends. I used a cardboard square that had held a bolt of sequins. It was the perfect length.

As I removed each bunch of yarn, I glued it between two strips of fabric, and then glued the strips to the ball cap starting at the bottom edge. I continued to layer the strips up to the crown.

For some color, I added gold beads, Christmas trim, and strings of sequins here and there.

Mop Wig

The crown is separate and attached with a thin piece of elastic pulled under the yarn. See the mask section for the face.

Have you ever wondered how to keep one of those **Mop Wigs** on your head? You guessed it — glue it to a ball cap. Actually, I used two cotton mops, dyed red, and glued them to a cap with the bill removed.

> **T I P** Wash the ball cap before using. Place it on a wig head or styrofoam head to dry. This will keep the wrinkles out.

Wedding Skullcaps

Wedding skullcaps are thin white mesh caps with wire around the edges that cover the skull. They are used to build wedding veils on. If you're lucky, or watch closely, you can find them in thrift shops. If you can't, go to a wedding supply store. These are not an expensive item.

The problem with the skullcaps is that the mesh is quite delicate and tears easily. They are made from very light fabric and trim. To use them for a showgirl headpiece, I first apply a coat of Sculptural Arts Coating. This gives the cap the texture and strength needed to build the headpiece.

Showgirl Headpiece #1

Showgirl Headpiece #1

Making the Hat

1. Coat the skullcap with Sculptural Arts Coating. Let dry.

2. Glue white appliques from the bodice of a wedding dress to the skullcap, leaving a space in back for the feathers.

3. Glue black and white feathers to the inside of a large white applique, then glue the applique to the back of the skullcap.

4. Glue strings of rhinestones to the quills of the long feathers. If you don't have rhinestones, use drops of glitter fabric paint for a similar look.

Showgirl Headpiece #2

Showgirl
Headpiece #2

Making the Hat

1. Glue a chunk of Styrofoam to the top of the skullcap.

2. Apply a coat of Sculptural Arts Coating — be sure to coat the Styrofoam heavily. Let dry.

3. Push the feather quills into the Styrofoam and glue well.

4. Glue strings of gold sequins onto the skullcap to cover it and around the Styrofoam.

5. Glue gold Christmas beads around the edge of the Styrofoam, leaving them hanging down.

Showgirl Headpiece #3

Showgirl Headpiece #3

Making the Hat

1. Glue a chunk of Styrofoam onto the left side of the skullcap.

2. Apply a coat of Sculptural Arts Coating. Make it thick around and over the Styrofoam. Let dry.

3. Cover the entire skullcap with black lace. I used a thin layer of Sculptural Arts Coating over the lace to hold it on. Glue is too messy with holey lace. Let dry.

4. Apply gold glitter fabric paint wherever there are holes in the lace. Let dry.

5. Stick the quills of the feathers into the sides of the Styrofoam from both sides. Glue well.

6. Add more black lace between the feathered sections and apply gold glitter fabric paint where the holes are. Let dry.

7. Glue on lightweight black strung beads so they hang from the feathered section.

Butterfly Headpiece

Butterfly Headpiece

Making the Hat

1. Glue a chunk of styrofoam onto each side of the skullcap.

2. Apply a coat of Sculptural Arts Coating. Make it thick around and over the Styrofoam. Let dry.

3. Cover the entire skullcap with black sequins. I used a thin layer of Sculptural Arts Coating over the sequins. Let dry.

4. Stick the quills of the feathers into the styrofoam on each side. Glue well.

5. Add more black sequins around the feathered sections.

Note: Because this is a showgirl headpiece for a butterfly costume, the feathers should appear to be antennas.

T I P As with the ball caps, if the headpiece is going to be heavy or pull to one side, attach an elastic chinstrap to both sides before beginning.

Headbands and Visors

When using a headband to make a headpiece, you're better off using the more expensive ones that have padding and cloth covering. They will be less prone to break, and the glue adheres better to the fabric. That's not to say you cannot use the cheaper plastic ones — they will work, but the others are better.

When I say I'm using a headband, it is the more expensive type. I have done everything from a Cleopatra headpiece to devil horns with headbands. (See examples.)

Cleopatra Headpiece

Cleopatra Headpiece

Making the Headpiece

1. Cut two sections of lightweight cardboard into the desired shape. Glue gold oilcloth to both sides of each piece. Glue the two pieces together.

2. Glue the cardboard section to the underside of the headband at the center, then make it stand up folding it backward and gluing it to the front edge of the headband.

3. Decorate the cardboard with drops of fabric paint and large, lightweight plastic pieces. The ones I used were from a beaded curtain.

4. Glue more beads from the curtain directly to the headband on both sides, leaving them hanging down. Glue beads to the back, behind the cardboard piece, and leave them hanging down.

TIP When using hanging beads on a headband, be conscious of the weight. Light plastic beads are best.

Dolly Headpiece

Dolly Headpiece

Making the Headpiece

1. Use a wide, black fabric headband. Cut the quills of the feathers off flush with the feather part.

2. Glue the feathers to the back of the headband, some going up, others down.

3. Glue strings of gold sequins to the quills of long feathers.

4. Glue red and black maribu feathers to the top of the headband and along the back to cover where the feathers are glued on.

Saloon Girl Headpiece

Saloon Girl Headpiece

Making the Headpiece

1. Use a hot pink fabric headband.

2. Start on one side, whichever side you want the feathers to hang down farthest, and glue feathers on in layers until you reach the other side. Use the longer feathers where you want them to hang down farther.

3. Add a bit of sequin trim or perhaps a flower if desired.

Kitty Headpiece #1

Making the Headpiece

1. Use a wide, black fabric headband. Cut two pieces of foam in the shape of cat ears. Glue pink satin to the front of the ears, black fur to the back, and trim them with sequins. Glue the ears to either side of the headband.

2. Glue black feathers to the back of the headband.

3. Glue black sequin trim to the top of headband and to the back to cover up where the feathers are glued on and to help hold them up.

4. Add a bit of white maribu to the center of the headband between the ears.

Kitty Headpiece #1

Kitty Headpiece #2

This was a costume I made for myself years ago. It was lightweight, comfortable, and filled the bill for Halloween.

Making the Headpiece

1. Use a wide, black fabric headband.

2. Cut two pieces of foam in the shape of cat ears. Glue on black fur to cover the foam and glue the ears to either side of the headband. Trim the ears with rhinestones, fabric paint, or sequins.

3. Add one tall, black feather, gluing it to the headband behind one ear. With the black curly wig and a bit of makeup, this headpiece makes a great cat.

Kitty Headpiece #2

Devil Headpiece

You might think it is easy to find a set of devil horns to purchase, but what if you need them and it's not Halloween? Making them is easy.

Making the Headpiece

1. Use a wide, red fabric headband. Cut two pieces of foam in the shape of horns. Glue string sequin trim around the horns till they are covered.

2. Glue horns to red headband.

3. Glue red sequins on top of headband and around and under where horns are glued on. This will stabilize them and hold them on better. (See mask and jewelry sections for more accessories.)

Devil Headpiece

Using a visor is similar to using a headband. By standing a visor upright on the head, it can be used for some interesting headpieces.

Cancan Headpiece

Cancan Headpiece

Making the Headpiece

1. Stand the visor upright. Glue on bronze sequin trim to cover the front. Glue a bow on the front.

2. Glue colorful ruffles on the back. Glue on feathers.

Flowered Headpiece

Flowered Headpiece

Making the Headpiece

1. Stand the visor upright. Glue multicolored ribbons down each side, leaving them to hang.

2. Glue multicolored silk flowers to both sides of the visor.

TIP Use cloth visors instead of plastic. The glue will adhere better, and they will stand up just as well as the plastic ones because the glue helps them become stiffer.

Witch Hats

Sometimes a simple object can be a godsend in a pinch. One day I needed a black, large-brimmed hat in a hurry and found I didn't have much to work with in the shop. My gaze landed on a witch's hat — the brim in particular. It was black, it was wide — it might work.

Large-Brimmed Black Hat

Large-Brimmed
Black Hat

Making the Hat

1. Coat the underside of the brim with Sculptural Arts Coating to make it more solid and prevent it from fraying when cut. Let dry.

2. Cut the pointed crown out.

3. Run a long piece of non-fray black fabric over the hole where the crown was and into two slots cut out of either side of the hole, leaving the ends long enough to tie under the chin.

4. Glue green sequins and silver beads onto the brim. Glue peacock feathers on and add a silver, beaded broach to the quills.

Spider Web Hat

When making a giant spider illusion, I needed a showgirl hat that resembled a spider web. The brim of a witch's hat worked perfectly.

Spider Web Hat

Making the Hat

1. Coat one side of the brim with Sculptural Arts Coating. Let dry.

2. Cut the pointed crown out. Lay the brim flat.

3. Draw a spider web on the brim with a white chalk pencil. Glue rhinestones over the lines you drew to make the web. You can substitute glitter fabric paint or sequin trim.

4. Cut the holes out between the web.

5. Glue the web to one side of a woman's felt hat.

6. Glue rhinestone trim around the edge of the hat.

7. Glue feathers behind the web and a few more in the front.

Siamese Showgirl

Siamese Showgirl

When I needed a Siamese showgirl headpiece, I used a set of angel wings painted black.

Making the Headpiece

1. Start with a woman's black felt hat with a brim. Cut off the brim, but save it to make the mask.

2. Spray paint the white angel wings black. Bend them to the desired shape and glue them to the top of the hat.

3. At the very top of the wings, glue on a piece of the hat brim.

4. Glue gold and black beaded fringe to the edges of the wings. Glue gold and red sequin trim to cover where the beaded fringe was glued on.

5. Glue a black curly wig to the back of the hat and a short length of beaded fringe to the center of the front.

T I P   Look for cocktail dresses with beaded fringe that is sewn on in strips. Lamp fringe works well, too.

Eliza Hat

Gothic Headpiece

Felt Hats

When I think of a woman's black felt hat, I'm reminded of **Eliza Dolittle** in *My Fair Lady*. I recently made the costume from the first act. It is still relatively easy to find women's felt hats in thrift shops, antique stores, and occasionally at a rummage sale. I purchase them where and when I can. By gluing some silk flowers on the hat, my Eliza was ready to go. (See Eliza Hat.)

A black, felt pillbox hat was a wonderful beginning for my **Gothic Headpiece.** I safety-pinned black ribbed trim to each side, allowing enough to fit under the chin, and glued a piece of black felt inside to cover the pins. After gluing a sheer scarf so it hung from the crown, I decorated the hat with gold Christmas beads, black iridescent sequins, buttons, and fabric paint. (See Gothic Headpiece.)

My **Elizabethan Headpiece** was born from a small-brimmed, black felt hat. I cut the brim off, cut the brim in half, and glued one half to the crown of the hat so it stands up. I glued trim around the edges and in front, glued a sheer scarf so it hangs from the center of the crown, and added a stiff white ruffle to the piece of brim that sticks up. (See Elizabethan Headpiece.)

Elizabethan
Headpiece

TIP

As long as you glue trim around the edge, the felt will hold together quite well.

Starting with a large-brimmed hat and using the same method as I used for the Elizabethan Headpiece, I created the **African Princess Headpiece.** I cut the brim from the crown and glued all but one small section of it to the top of the crown so it would stand up. Then I glued the small section to the top of the brim piece. I glued wide trim around the edge of the crown and decorated the hat with lightweight hanging beads. I added two strips of rhinestones on the front for accent. If you used gold beads, this would also make a wonderful **Egyptian Headpiece.** (See African Princess Headpiece.)

African Princess
Headpiece

After cutting the brim off a black felt hat, I coated the crown with Sculptural Arts Coating, then cut it in the shape of a **Crown** for my knight. Next I decorated with plastic jewels and fabric paint and placed the crown over a chain mail hood and collar made of gold sequin fabric. (See Knight Crown.)

Knight Crown

Matador Hats are not easy to come by. Unless you have a specific place to purchase them, they must be made. Cut the brim off a black felt hat with a rounded crown. Coat the crown with Sculptural Arts Coating while it's pulled down over a wig head. That will give you the rounded look at the top. Let dry. Cut a hole in each side and cut two pieces from the brim. Bend the pieces into shape, push the ends through the hole, and glue them to the inside of the hat. Coat them with Sculptural Arts Coating and let dry. Glue a piece of black trim underneath each side so the hat fits snuggly. Decorate with colorful fabric paint or trim. (See Matador Hat.)

Matador Hat

Need a hat for a **Storybook Prince?** Start with a black felt hat. Leaving the brim down, glue a circle of fabric onto it where the brim meets the crown. Take tucks to give it that puffy look. Once the fabric is glued on, glue a piece of trim around the edge to finish. Turn the brim up higher on one side than the

Prince Hat

other. Glue the lower edge to the inside of the crown at the point where it connects to the brim so it won't come up. I decorated the brim with black iridescent sequins and gold appliques and glued feathers to one side of the back. (See Prince Hat.)

Top Hat

If you happen to need a nice, black felt **Top Hat** and cannot locate one, there's a way to make one that looks pretty good. You've seen those foam top hats, usually striped in different colors — that will be your start. Tuck the fabric in where the brim is sewn to the crown to make it the height you want. Glue the crown to the brim. Next, you will need to cut four pieces of black felt to cover the hat: one for the top of the crown, one for the sides, and one each for the top and bottom of the brim. Before cutting, use a white chalk pencil to mark out the pieces on the felt. You may wish to trace around the hat. Glue felt onto the underside of the brim first and coat it with Sculptural Arts Coating. Let dry. Place the hat over a jar that fits snuggly and coat the entire hat. Let dry. Glue felt on crown and top of brim. Let dry. Trim with strips of black felt. (See Top Hat.)

Plastic and Paper Hats

Cigarette Girl Hat

There is so much plastic around today, you won't have trouble finding some to use for hats. You can purchase cheap plastic hats at party supply stores, costume shops, and during Halloween, at discount stores, fabric shops, and even drug stores. You might think plastic is difficult to work with because it breaks so easily, but what if I told you I could make plastic bend? No, I'm not Superwoman — I just use Sculptural Arts Coating on it and it becomes pliable.

Bell Girl Hat

After coating a plastic top hat and letting it dry, I can cut the top out and use it as a pillbox hat. If you don't have a plastic top hat, you can do the same with the bottom of a plastic bottle. Then glue your fabric on, coat it again, and trim it. You'll be amazed what you can come up with. (See Cigarette Girl Hat and Bell Girl Hat.)

TIP Because plastic slips around on the head, glue a strip of foam to the inside edge.

When creating costumes for *The King and I,* I had very little time and a lot of **Siamese Headpieces** to make. To begin, I coated a stack of old plastic top hats with Sculptural Arts Coating and cut the tops out. That was my base. I glued a piece of thin elastic over the top and stretched it under the chin to hold the hat on. Using chunks of foam, also coated, I built up the hat, ending with a pointed piece at the top. I spray painted the whole thing gold, then glued on Christmas beads, small iridescent garland, and gold sequins to enhance. I finished it off with drops of gold glitter fabric paint. (See Siamese Headpiece.)

Siamese
Headpiece

How to create that wonderful transparent crown for **Glenda the Good Witch** was a puzzler. As I sat in my shop looking around, my gaze landed on a poster of *The Wizard of Oz.* It wasn't the picture that intrigued me, but the large piece of plastic covering it. I retrieved it and coated both sides with Sculptural Arts Coating. I let it dry. With a Magic Marker, I marked what I needed from the plastic and cut it out with a pair of those Chinese scissors — you know, the ones that cut anything. It worked. I glued it together in the back and decorated it with sequins and a sequin applique. I think it turned out great. (See Glenda Crown.)

Glenda Crown

Speaking of **Crowns,** there are times when there is not one handy and very little to make one from. I took a hat brim and glued gold sequins and trim to it, added a red, silky drape, and created the crown look with that gold wire with little gold stars hanging from it. I can't tell you how simple this is. (See Guenevere Crown.)

Guenevere
Crown

Cover a wedding veil base with sequins for a **Fairy.** Add flowers in back. (See Fairy Headpiece.)

Like plastic, paper hats are pretty easy to find. I use a lot of hats from New Year's Eve products. They come in all shapes and sizes, including one-size-fits-all, and they can be very colorful.

Fairy Headpiece

There are always patriotic events going on and cheap, paper **Patriotic Hats.** I found an Uncle Sam-style top hat for one of my patriotic projects. Because I didn't want the hat to tear, I coated it with Sculptural Arts Coating inside and out. The design was already there, so all I had to do was follow it with sequin trim. I added some red sequin star appliques and red feathers to finish the hat. (See Patriotic Top Hat.)

Patriotic Top Hat

Elton John Hat

Twine Boater

Rope Boater

Woman's
Medieval Hat

Elton John? You've got to be kidding. They wanted the old Elton John from the late '70s to early '80s. He was still glitzing it up pretty well back then. I had a gold New Year's Eve hat made of cardboard. It might work. I coated it inside and out with Sculptural Arts Coating and let it dry. Next, I glued a band on and glued purple sequin trim around the crown and brim until the entire hat was covered. I glued a feather on the side, added a mask, and called him Elton John. (See Elton John Hat.)

One of the hats that is asked for a great deal and used in many productions is a man's 1920s **Boater.** A nice one is expensive to purchase, if you can find it, and the plastic

T I P Like plastic, paper doesn't fit everyone well and tends to slip. Glue a strip of foam inside.

ones are really tacky looking — but easy to find and cheap to buy. I figured out a way to use the plastic boater and make it look like the more expensive one. After coating the plastic with Sculptural Arts Coating, let it dry and glue twine or small rope around it, beginning at the crown, until covered. It takes a bit of time, but is worth the effort. When covered, coat the hat again. Let dry. (See Twine Boater and Rope Boater.)

In addition to plastic and paper hats, you can also use plastic bottles. How beautiful can you make the bottom of a plastic bottle? Very pretty with a bit of fabric, trim, glue, and imagination. First and foremost, pick a bottle that will fit the wearer's head properly and wash it well. When completely dry, coat it with Sculptural Arts Coating on the outside. Let dry and cut the bottom out to the desired size.

Coat the inside and cover it with felt and a strip of foam for comfort. Next, cover the outside with fabric and coat again. Let dry. I used strips of fur, gold beads, a sheer scarf and ruffle in the back, and a large gold pin at the center. (See Woman's Medieval Hat.)

The same type of hat can be accomplished by using a squared crown from a straw hat or a felt hat. But, if you don't have them handy, the bottle works as well.

Fabric Hats

When working with fabric hats, consider the type of fabric required. Will it need to drape? If so, stay away from heavy or stiff fabrics. Some hats will need more body to them. When possible, I use leftover fabric from the original garments I used to make the rest of the costume. Some fabric hats require a base hat underneath. I use whatever works.

Man's Gothic Hat #1

Making the Hat

1. Begin with a collapsible foam clown hat.

2. Cut a circle of purple robe fabric and glue it on where the brim meets the crown, taking tucks here and there to give it that puffy look.

3. Lay the hat on the same fabric and cut out a circle as wide as the brim. Glue it on to cover the brim, starting on the underside of the brim and tucking where needed.

4. Glue feathers and a jewel onto one side.

Man's Gothic Hat #1

Man's Gothic Hat #2

Making the Hat

1. Double your chosen fabric and cut two identical circles.

2. With the circles wrong side out, glue or sew them together along the edges, leaving a small area open to turn the fabric. Turn right side out and glue the small area closed.

3. Optional: Sew a piece of elastic around the crown, stretching it as you go. Leave a healthy-sized brim. You can also glue the elastic on, taking tucks here and there until the hat is the correct size for the wearer.

4. Glue feathers and a gold button on one side.

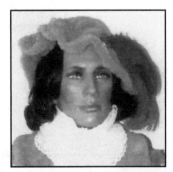

Man's Gothic Hat #2

Renaissance
Woman's Hat

When in need of a **Renaissance Woman's Hat,** I came up with a simple but attractive idea. I had a black cocktail dress with large, stiff, puffy sleeves made of netting. I cut a sleeve out of the dress and glued it to the inside of a piece of wide, beaded trim large enough to fit around a head. I glued a jewel in the center of the front. (See Renaissance Woman's Hat.)

Renaissance Man's Hat

Renaissance Man's Hat

Making the Hat

1. Cut the sleeve out of a thin, figured robe.

2. Add a bit of stuffing, but not much. Twist the sleeve around tightly and wrap gold sequins to hold it. Glue them in place.

3. Cut a circle out of the same fabric. Glue it inside the twisted sleeve, making tucks to give it a puffy look.

4. At the back of the hat, between the crown and the brim, glue feathers hanging down.

5. Glue a piece of blue fabric and a blue jewel to the opposing side of the front.

Hansel Hat

One of the easiest hats to make is the **Robin Hood-Style Hat.** It is merely two rectangular pieces of fabric glued together at the edges on three sides, wrong side out. Turn it right side out and decorate for the desired look. (See Hansel Hat, Robin Hood Hat, Prince Hat, and Carhop Hats #1 and #2.)

T I P
If you tack a small loop of thin elastic on each side of these hats, it is easier to secure them to the wearer's hair with bobby pins.

Robin Hood Hat

Prince Hat

Carhop Hat #1

Carhop Hat #2

Glenda Hat *(The Wiz)*

You've seen the Glenda Hat made of plastic. Now I'll show you Glenda from *The Wiz* made of foam and fabric.

Making the Hat

1. Cut a piece of 3/4" foam to the desired shape.

2. Coat the back side with Sculptural Arts Coating and press a solid-colored fabric into it. Let dry.

3. Glue glitzy fabric to the front, overlapping about an inch onto the back. Glue trim around edges on inside to give it that finished look.

4. Glue the sides together in back to form hat.

5. Decorate with beads, sequins, and a sequin applique at the point, in the center, and around the forehead.

Glenda Hat (The Wiz)

Egyptian Headpiece

For the Egyptian Headpiece, you must use a fabric that hangs well — not too limp, but not too stiff. To measure the length of fabric, drape it over the head and make sure it falls to the desired length on both sides. The method below can be used for male and female Egyptian headpieces. You would simply decorate them differently.

When making a female version, you might want to hang some gold Christmas beads along the sides and back to give it a more feminine look. Make sure the edges of the fabric are either glued under or trimmed to keep them from fraying, or use a non-fray fabric.

I chose the ball cap for a base because it is adjustable in the back.

Making the Headpiece

1. You can use any round crown for a base. I used a ball cap with the bill cut off.

2. The fabric is fluid, blue sequin. Make sure it's wide enough to hang down to the neck in the back. Glue the middle of the fabric to the front and sides of a ball cap.

3. Glue a strip of wide trim over where the fabric is glued to the cap. The fabric should hang naturally.

4. You can spot glue fabric at top of crown to make sure it's secure.

5. Decorate the front with gold appliques and a broach.

Egyptian Headpiece

Chapter 5 # Big Heads

Many productions are inspired by popular movies. When *The Little Mermaid* came out, it seemed all the schools wanted to do an undersea production. The first time I made the costumes for such a production, they wanted undersea creatures with open faces and lightweight heads.

I love working with fur. It can be found in many colors, glues to itself probably better than any other fabric, and doesn't have to be hemmed. Even so, making fur heads with open faces that weren't too heavy was a challenge.

Sebastian the Lobster

For Sebastian the Lobster, I started with a ball cap to build on.

Sebastian the Lobster

Making the Head

1. Cut the bill off a ball cap and tack a wide elastic strap to each side to fit under the chin snugly.

2. Shape a piece of 1" foam like the crown of a top hat and glue it to the ball cap.

3. Glue red fur on the cap, leaving about an inch along the edge uncovered to glue strips of fur on for the sides.

4. Beginning on one side, glue a wide strip of fur to the bottom edge of the ball cap. Leave the front open. The strip of fur must be long enough to make a skirt at the neck that covers the tops of the shoulders.

5. Slit the fur up the back to above the skirt. Glue a red shoestring around the neck, pulling the fur in and leaving enough length in the back to tie it.

6. Cover a flap of foam with fur and glue it to the front for the mouth.

7. Using small pieces of white and black fur, make the eyes and eyebrows. I covered half of a plastic egg for each eye.

8. Glue wire antennas onto the forehead, then glue a small piece of red fur over the ends to hold them in place.

9. Make large eyelids from red fur and wrap around the eyes.

10. Trim with gold fabric paint.

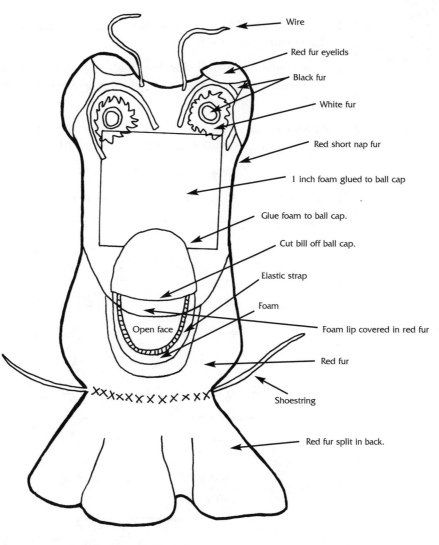

Sebastian the Lobster

Seahorse

Because the seahorse head is rounded at the top, I considered using a plastic ball, but it could be a problem when washing, so I had to come up with another way to make the rounded look.

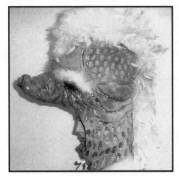

Seahorse

Making the Head

1. Start with a fabric hood that ties under the chin. I took one off a spring jacket. Glue a tuck in the top so it fits well.

2. Make a firm ball of fiberfill, coat it with spray adhesive, and let dry. Glue it to the top of the hood.

3. Glue a piece of foam shaped like a nose to the front of the hood above the opening for the face.

4. Cover head with gold fur, leaving a bit hanging below the bottom of the hood. Cover a shoestring with fur and sew or pin it on to the front of the neck for a tie.

5. Make eyelids of fur and lashes of white maribu and glue in place. The eyes are drawn with blue glitter fabric paint.

6. Glue a white feather boa from the front of the head down the back.

7. Add the tip of the nose and other decoration with gold fabric paint.

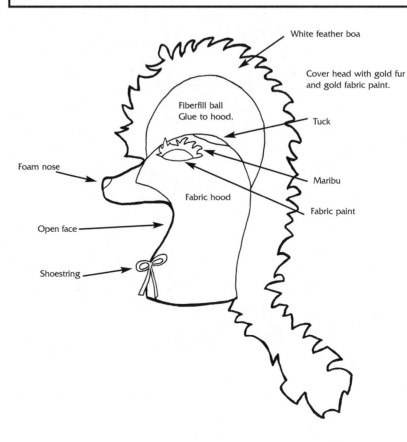

Octopus

When making an octopus, one must consider balance. It will be important for the person wearing it, especially with all those arms hanging down on all sides. I found a brown hooded sweatshirt to build on.

Octopus

Making the Head

1. Cut the sweatshirt off around the shoulders.

2. Glue 2" foam over the hood and the collar.

3. Make a big ball of fiberfill and spray it with adhesive. Let it dry and glue it to the top of the head, pulling it around to the sides and back.

4. Glue on brown fur to cover the head.

5. Cut eight strips of 4" foam. I used one of those pieces of foam people put on their beds.

6. Lay a piece of foam on the fur and cut out a piece of fur large enough to cover it on all sides. Leave four extra inches at one end. Glue fur to the foam arm and glue the end with the extra four inches shut. Repeat for all eight.

7. I used glue and large pins to attach the eight arms to the collar. Attach them using the four extra inches at the end of each. Glue brown fur over the collar to hide where the arms are attached.

8. Split the collar, fur, and hood to the base of the skull between two of the arms in the back. Glue a brown shoestring to the front and bring it around the neck so it ties in the back.

9. Make eyelids of brown fur and glue them over large eyes of white and black fur. Eyebrows are black fur.

10. Add suction cups to the arms with circles of fabric paint.

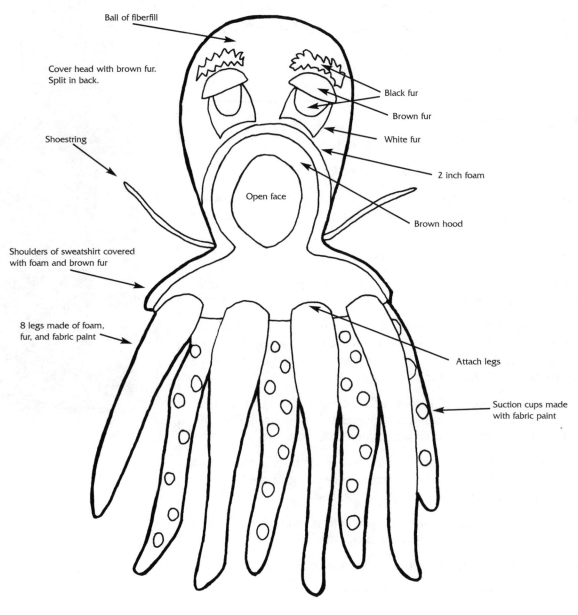

Ball of fiberfill

Cover head with brown fur.
Split in back.

Black fur

Brown fur

White fur

Shoestring

2 inch foam

Open face

Brown hood

Shoulders of sweatshirt covered
with foam and brown fur

8 legs made of foam,
fur, and fabric paint

Attach legs

Suction cups made
with fabric paint

Octopus

Eel

The eel was an interesting challenge. Because I needed a snakeskin look, I didn't want to use fur. I found some upholstery fabric that was exactly the right color.

Eel

Making the Head

1. Cut the bill off a ball cap and tack an elastic chinstrap to each side.

2. Glue a 2" piece of foam across the top of the cap, leaving six inches hanging down on each side.

3. Shape the head from a chunk of thick foam and glue it on the top of the 2" foam. Add a piece of foam for the bottom lip.

4. Glue red satin fabric inside the open mouth.

5. At the back of the ball cap, glue a piece of upholstery to hang down the back and past the feet to drag along the floor.

6. Cut a U out of the top of another strip of upholstery and glue it to the sides of the cap, so the U forms an opening for the face, and the strip hangs down just below the crotch. With a piece of Velcro, attach a wide piece of elastic from the bottom edge of the front flap, between the legs to the back.

7. Cover the head with upholstery, overlapping the upholstery fabric to the sides and back.

8. I cut a ruffle off a piece of netting taken from inside a pink dress and glued it from the top of the head down the back.

9. Make the eyes from pieces of gold fabric. Paint the slit in the center using black fabric paint.

10. The design is made with gold fabric paint.

**T
I
P**   Be sure you leave the neck big enough to slip over the head.

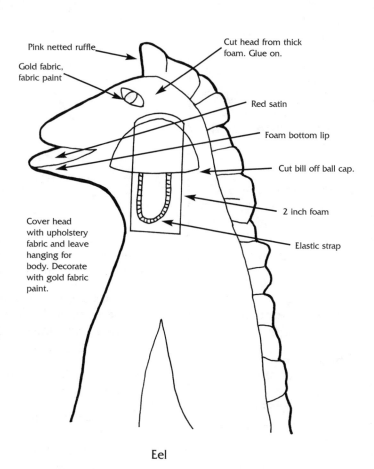

Pink netted ruffle

Gold fabric, fabric paint

Cut head from thick foam. Glue on.

Red satin

Foam bottom lip

Cut bill off ball cap.

2 inch foam

Elastic strap

Cover head with upholstery fabric and leave hanging for body. Decorate with gold fabric paint.

Eel

Frog

Frog

The Frog Costume needed to have a really big head. I started with a felt hat that fit snugly on the head, some thick foam, and green fur to get the desired effect.

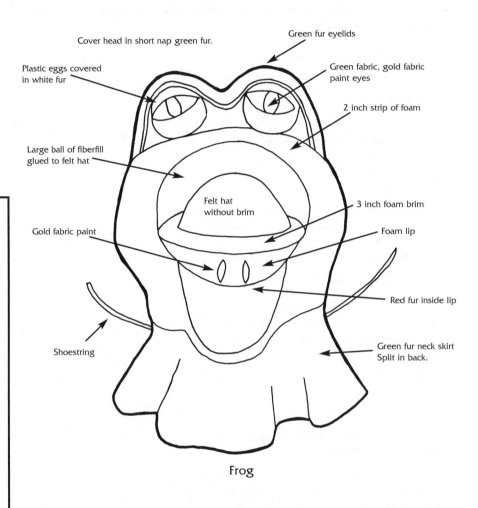

Cover head in short nap green fur.

Green fur eyelids

Plastic eggs covered in white fur

Green fabric, gold fabric paint eyes

2 inch strip of foam

Large ball of fiberfill glued to felt hat

Gold fabric paint

Felt hat without brim

3 inch foam brim

Foam lip

Red fur inside lip

Shoestring

Green fur neck skirt Split in back.

Frog

Making the Costume

1. Use only the crown of the felt hat and make sure it fits the head well. Make a large brim of 3" foam that goes all the way around the hat.

2. Make a ball of fiberfill and spray it with adhesive, then let it dry before gluing it to the top of the hat.

3. Glue a wide strip of 2" foam across the top of the fiberfill ball, leaving six inches hanging down on both sides.

4. Glue one half of a plastic egg to the top of the foam on either side so they face forward.

5. Add a large foam lip and cover the front of the face with short nap green fur. Cover the inside of the lip with red fur.

6. Glue white fur over the egg halves.

7. Drape a piece of short nap green fur over the head and tops of the eyes. Make sure the piece of fur is long enough to make a collar and wide enough to cover the back. Glue it on, then glue it together under the chin.

8. Split the fur open in back and glue a green shoestring around the neck from the front to the back, leaving enough to tie.

9. Glue green glitter fabric onto the eyes and use gold fabric paint to make the pupils. Add the nose holes and line the eyelids with gold fabric paint.

Turtle

I couldn't make the turtle with upholstery fabric or fur because I wanted a slick look. I considered felt, but it's hard to cover things well with felt. The turtle also has a smaller head. I had to put my thinking cap on for this one. As I sat gazing around the shop considering my options, my gaze rested on an old astronaut helmet. The shape was right, the size was right — but, how to cover it? The answer lay in fur and Sculptural Arts Coating.

Turtle

Helmet

Making the Costume

1. Remove the shield from the astronaut helmet.

2. To add height, glue just a bit of fiberfill to the top and spray it with adhesive. Let dry.

3. Make the lip with a 1/2" piece of foam so it hangs over the opening a bit.

4. Glue green fur on to cover the head, lip, and the neck of the helmet. It doesn't matter if you put it on in pieces. To hide the seams, apply a thin strip of glue and push the fur into it from both sides.

5. Cut eyelids of fur and glue them on above where you want the eyes.

6. Cover the head with an even coating of Sculptural Arts Coating, pressing the fur down with your brush.

7. Glue on white and black felt eyes and two pieces of black felt for the nose holes and coat them.

8. Add a piece of foam inside the helmet if needed to make it fit more snuggly.

T I P   Because of the coating, the outside of the turtle head cannot be washed, although it can be wiped off with a damp rag.

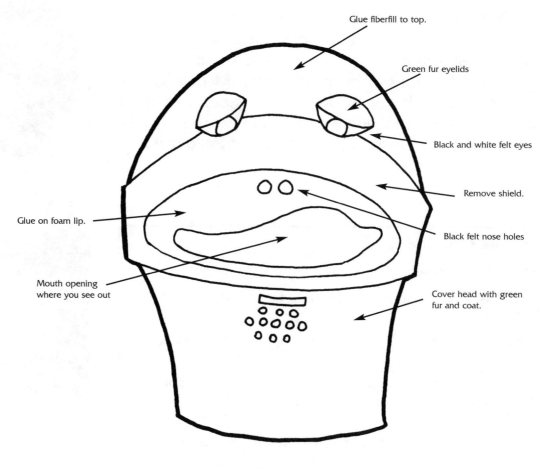

Glue fiberfill to top.

Green fur eyelids

Black and white felt eyes

Remove shield.

Glue on foam lip.

Black felt nose holes

Mouth opening
where you see out

Cover head with green
fur and coat.

Turtle

OK, you're saying, *I have the head, now what do I do about a turtle shell?* You know those slightly domed, plastic sleds kids used in the winter? Turn one upside down, cut the handles off, cover it with fur, and coat. Cover the back piece of plastic armor with fur. Leave the fur long enough to reach the crotch. Tack two pieces of wide elastic to the fabric. Pull the elastic between the legs and hook it to the inside of the covered sled with Velcro. You can wear black sweats or tights and a long-sleeved muscle shirt beneath. To complete the costume, add hands and feet. Use the ideas for making animal feet from the chapter on feet, shoes, and leggings.

Turkey

After I discovered how well the astronaut helmets worked for heads, there was no stopping me. They were fast, easy, durable, and could be cleaned inside. What more could one want? The problem for the average individual is that he or she will probably have to purchase the helmet through a costume shop. Schools and people involved with theatre and parades can order them directly from costume companies.

Turkey

When the weatherman from a local television channel requested a turkey head for the Thanksgiving parade, I made one using a helmet, and he rented it every year for many years. Another costumer in Texas saw my turkey and wanted one, so I made another and sold it to her.

Making the Head

1. Remove the plastic shield from the face of the helmet. Glue four layers of red netting across the outside of the opening.

2. Glue some fiberfill to the top of the helmet to make it taller. Spray it with adhesive and let dry.

3. Shape a beak from 1/2" foam. Cover the inside with red fur and the outside with orange fabric. Cut two pieces of red fur into the shape of a waddle (that red thing on the beak) and glue them to each other. Coat the waddle with Sculptural Arts Coating for that slick look. Make the nose holes on the beak of black felt and fabric paint.

4. Cover the head with brown fur and leave enough hanging down the front for a neck.

5. Glue strips of red fur around the beak to cover where the brown fur connects to the beak.

6. Glue pieces of white fur onto the head for the eyes and coat. Draw in the irises with black and gold fabric paint.

7. Glue on two pieces of fur for the eyelids and trim the edges with fabric paint.

8. For the final touch and to give it that feathered look, I glued on a natural brown turkey boa to cover top and back of the head.

Although no one will be able to see inside, whoever wears the head will see through the netting where the corners of the beak are. This turkey has been an absolute hit everywhere he's gone.

Wizard

Wizard

Using the astronaut helmet to make a human character presented a challenge. It is not always easy to create that wonderful skin effect one desires with a person costume. Due to the recent popularity of the Harry Potter books and movies, I had to have a Wizard costume.

Making the Costume

1. Start with an astronaut helmet. Remove the blue face shield and cover the opening with four layers of white netting.

2. Build the top of the head using fiberfill and spray adhesive. When you do this, be sure you really pack the fiberfill tight so it will stay up.

3. Using pale pink stretch terry, cover a piece of foam in the shape of a nose and glue it in place.

4. Glue stretch terry to the bottom edge of the front of the helmet half way around. Stretch it up over the face, gluing where needed, (e.g., around the nose) until you cover the fiberfill. Glue the terry to the back of the helmet to hold it in place. You don't need to worry about the back and sides because they will be covered with hair.

5. Cut out the mouth, being careful not to cut the netting.

6. Make eyes from pieces of white, blue, and black felt and glue them in place. Make eyelids from pieces of terry fabric stretched over thin felt and use thin strips of black fur for eyelashes.

7. Coat the face, eyes, and eyelids with Sculptural Arts Coating and let dry.

8. I glued the fabric and blue sequin trim to a black satin witch's hat, leaving extra fabric at the top so it would hang over. Glue a tassel to the point.

9. I used old Santa wigs and beards to make the hair, a mustache, and bushy eyebrows. If you don't have hair, substitute long nap white fur.

10. The final touch was a pair of glasses made of gold glitter pipe cleaners. Twist them together until they are long enough to shape into glasses. Glue them to the face. Glue a single string of gold sequins to the front of the frames.

11. I added a piece of foam inside the head to make it more stable on the wearer's head.

Whoopi Goldbear

How about combining animal and human characteristics in a head? Inspired by the collectable bears that resemble movie stars and famous people, I decided to do the same thing with costumes. My first was Whoopi Goldbear.

Whoopi Goldbear

Making the Head

1. Begin with an astronaut helmet with the shield removed and the top built higher with fiberfill and spray adhesive.

2. Glue four layers of black netting over the opening.

3. Shape the nose from foam and cover it with brown fur. Cover the face with brown fur and glue on the nose. Finish off the nose with black felt and fabric paint.

4. Make eyes out of pieces of white and black felt and coat. Eyelids are brown fur trimmed with black felt eyelashes.

5. Make teeth from a strip of thin foam covered with white felt and coated. Lips are coated red fur.

6. Decorate a pair of large red clown glasses with drops of fabric paint and glue them to the face.

7. Make dreadlocks from strips of black long nap fur glued to themselves in different lengths. Glue them to the head.

8. Shape ears from foam. Cover them with pink felt on the inside and brown fur on the outside, then glue them to the head between the dreadlocks.

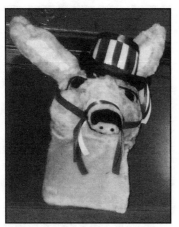

Donkey

Elephant

Donkey and Elephant Heads

To understand how to use foam to make a head, think of the petals of a flower closing at night. It's actually quite similar. Because I ran out of astronaut helmets, I was forced to make my Democratic Donkey and Republican Elephant from foam. It was election year and the parades were happening.

Making the Head

1. Using 1" foam, cut out four petals — they should be squared at the bottom, wide in the center, and pointed at the top. When glued together, they should form an opening at the bottom as big around as your head. Measure your head at the largest point and divide by four. That will be the length of the squared bottoms of your petals. Once you have all four petals cut out, glue each petal to the next along the edges, starting at the bottom.

2. For the donkey, cut a piece of foam for the nose. For the elephant, cut out a trunk. Glue them to the face before covering.

3. Determine where to place eyeholes by putting the head on and touching the outside with a marker where your eyes are. Remove the head and cut the eyes the size you desire. Cover them with four layers of netting from the outside.

4. Cover the head with fur. If your fur is too heavy, you will need to use a thicker foam for the nose. I used a lightweight gray fur. Leave enough fur hanging down the front and back of the head to tuck inside the costume. Or you can glue a piece to the inside of the opening.

5. Use black fabric paint on the center of the eye, keeping in mind that you must leave enough room to see out. Glue on eyelids of gray fur trimmed with strips of black fur.

6. Glue black short nap fur onto the ends of the noses.

7. Make ears from foam. On the donkey, cover the inside with pink fabric and the outside with gray fur. For the elephant, use gray fur inside and out. Glue the ears to the head and add a strip of fur around each ear to help secure it.

8. Make tusks for the elephant from foam. Cover them with white felt and glue them on, using a strip of fur to secure.

9. Decorate the heads with hats and red, white, and blue ribbon and feathers. This makes them look political.

10. If the head moves around too much, add a piece of foam inside the back.

Glue four foam "petals" together to form a round head.
Cover entire head with grey fur after completing form.

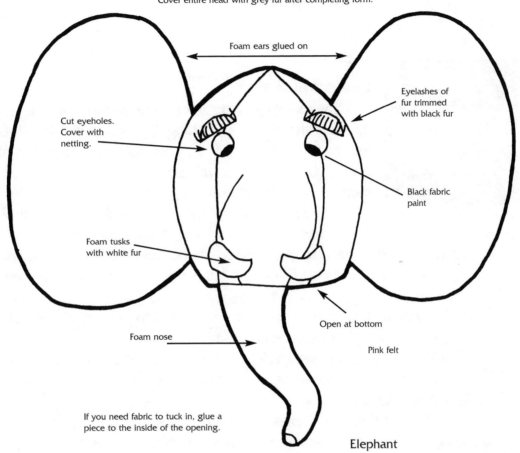

Foam ears glued on

Eyelashes of
fur trimmed
with black fur

Cut eyeholes.
Cover with
netting.

Black fabric
paint

Foam tusks
with white fur

Open at bottom

Foam nose

Pink felt

If you need fabric to tuck in, glue a
piece to the inside of the opening.

Elephant

Chapter 6 Masks

Original Masks

Basic Masks

Inexpensive, full white face masks can be purchased through the Oriental Trading Company by the dozen. (See reference section.) The cost breaks down to about fifty cents apiece. Coating these with Sculptural Arts Coating will prevent them from splitting or tearing when cut.

I begin by coating the inside of the mask and pressing a plain white paper towel into the coating while still wet. When it's dry, cut the mask to the desired shape and decorate. Even though the mask now has more body, you will still need to be conscious of the weight of any trim used.

If you wish to build about the mask, trim the rounded forehead off and glue on lightweight poster board in the desired shape.

These masks are wonderful for a masquerade scene in a production, for the person who simply wants to wear a mask with a gown or suit, and even for a Mardi Gras party or parade.

The first three examples show how to build a mask up with cardboard. First coat the inside of the mask with Sculptural Arts Coating. Press in a paper towel and let dry. Cut the bottom of the mask into the desired design. Cut a piece of cardboard or poster board into the shape you want and glue it onto the forehead of the mask. Decorate the mask and cardboard with lightweight trim. (See Mask #1–3.)

TIP If the mask fits too close to the eyes, glue a strip of foam to the inside just above each eyehole to hold it out.

Mask 1

Mask 2

Mask 3

Masks on a Stick

What about those wonderful masks on a stick? They can be accomplished easily. Using the same white mask, coat the inside, but don't line with a paper towel. Cut the mask to the desired design and add a cardboard extension on top.

For the stick, you'll be using a wooden dowel rod — not too big. I normally buy the smallest size. If it's too long, simply cut it off. If you cut it, glue the cut end to the mask.

Before you begin decorating the mask, you'll want to attach it to the stick. It's much harder to attach it once you're dealing with feathers and trim. On one side, glue the mask to the dowel rod. Cut a piece of white felt to fit the back of the mask, leaving a bit of extra fabric on the side where the mask is attached to the stick. Glue the felt to the edge of the mask and around the stick to add a bit more security in the hold. Coat the felt with Sculptural Arts Coating and let dry.

Mask on a Stick #1

Now it's time to decorate. The colors you use will depend on the costume or gown worn with the mask. I used feathers, strips of colorful maribu, sequin trim, fabric paint, and wide, multicolored strands of tinsel because my masks were to be used at a Mardi Gras parade and dance.

When you are using long plumes, it's nice to cover the stems with a strip of contrasting sequins. It gives them a much nicer look, especially on the ladies' masks.

Mask on a Stick #2

For those who don't wish to wear a mask but want one, these masks on a stick are a nice addition — and they can be hung on a wall later as a reminder of a lovely evening. (See Mask on a Stick #1 and #2.)

Showgirl Masks

Remember those wonderful showgirl headpieces in the hats and headpieces section? I built the headpieces on wedding skullcaps. If you desire a mask to go with that type of headpiece, there is a simple way to make one that's removable.

When making the headpiece, staple one side of a strip of Velcro to each side. The Velcro will be covered by hanging beads or applique. Coat a white full-face mask with Sculptural Arts Coating, let it dry, and cut it to the desired size. Use a full-face mask because you'll want the final product to be a bit bigger than a half mask.

Gold and White
Showgirl Mask

White Showgirl Mask

Wig Clown

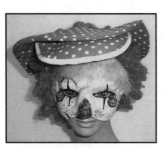

Hat Clown

Attach the other sides of the Velcro strips to the inside of the mask and decorate.

For the **Gold and White** beaded headpiece, I wanted a beaded look on the mask. After I stapled strips of Velcro to each side, leaving them long enough to attach to the Velcro on the headpiece, I decorated. I added drops of white fabric paint to get the beaded look I wanted and I trimmed the rest with gold sequins. (See Gold and White Showgirl Mask.)

For the **Black and White** showgirl headpiece, I needed a more elegant mask. After coating the inside of the mask with Sculptural Arts Coating and stapling Velcro to each side so it would attach to the headpiece, I covered the mask with wedding fabric and coated over it. This mask didn't need much decoration other than the wonderful wedding fabric. I did enhance above the eyes with drops of silver fabric paint. (See White Showgirl Mask.)

No Makeup Masks

Masks are a wonderful accessory for those who don't want to wear makeup or are unable to accomplish the look they want with makeup.

Clowns

Everybody loves a clown, and costuming for them is quite easy — except for the makeup. The basic white mask will work well as an alternative. Coat the inside of the mask with Sculptural Arts Coating and press a white paper towel into it while wet. Let dry. Glue a strip of foam over each eyehole if desired. Cut the mask to the desired size. If a wig is to be worn, you will want to trim off the large forehead.

For the first two clown examples, I mixed glitter in with Sculptural Arts Coating and coated the outside of the mask. Remember, the coating dries clear so the glitter will shine through. I cut the mouths off the masks because the people were going to a party where they would be eating and drinking. They added white makeup and red lipstick to their chins and mouths.

I decorated the masks with pieces of sequin appliques I cut up for the desired look and fabric paint. On the clown with the hat, I used some maribu. (See Wig Clown and Hat Clown.)

What if the clown doesn't want to wear a wig and hat or any makeup at all? I came up with a solution. Leave the mask full and follow the instructions above for coating the inside. Use red maribu for the hair and glue a lightweight plastic hat directly to the mask. Decorate the face with sequin trim and fabric paint. (See Cowboy Clown.)

Cowboy Clown

Ghost

I'm not sure everybody loves a ghost, but it can be a simple costume for those in need. I found some great ghost kits at a discount store. They included a plastic mask, a paintbrush, and some basic colored paints in little plastic containers. The instructions tell you to cut a hole in a sheet and glue it around the edge of the mask. Although the mask shapes are well done, it wouldn't look like much if you just followed the instructions.

Not being one who follows direction well, I came up with my own ideas. I coated the mask so it wouldn't tear or crack and glued a strip of foam near the top so it wouldn't slip around. These are large masks. I stapled a piece of Velcro to each side of the mask to hold it in place, enough to fit around the back of the head for more security.

Rather than use the paint in the package, I used fabric paint. It covered better and I could use the glitter paint where desired.

Instead of a sheet, I cut a long skirt out of a dress and glued the waist around the mask. It still needed something. Hair! I glued black maribu to cover where the skirt is attached to the mask. It defined the face, too, and gave it a bit more color. For the bottom half of the costume, I added a white flared nightdress. It was a comfortable, fun, and still unusual costume enhanced by the wonderful mask. (See Ghost Mask.)

Ghost Mask

Bride of Frankenstein

No makeup is needed for this Bride of Frankenstein. I used a white half mask with foam bolts glued on the sides and fabric paint enhancement, and the mask turned out great. (See Bride of Frankenstein.)

Bride of Frankenstein
Mask

Pink Woman Mask

Gold Man Mask

White Native
American Mask

Black Native
American Mask

Couples' Masks

Need masks for couples? Like the full-faced white masks, you can purchase a variety of colored masks the same way for about the same price. Before beginning, coat each mask with Sculptural Arts Coating, press paper towels into the inside while they are still wet, and glue strips of foam over each eyehole if desired. Then you're ready to cut.

Contrasting Couple

For my first couple, I chose a gold mask for the male and a pink one for the female. I saved some pieces I cut off the pink mask to add to the gold mask and vice versa. By adorning the gold mask with pink and the pink with gold, I made a wonderful contrasting couple. (See Pink Woman Mask and Gold Man Mask.)

Native American Couple

The second couple's masks are Native American. The couple had costumes, but they wanted something unusual to enhance them. After coating and cutting the masks, I glued a lightweight brown doe cloth over the man's mask, cut the eyeholes out, and decorated it with feathers, sequins, and fabric paint. I left the fabric long on each side so I could fringe it. Black maribu and white feathers hanging down finished the look. Even though this mask looks heavy, it is not, and it is very well balanced. The feathers are glued to a piece of lightweight poster board glued to the top of the mask. I think it gives it a wonderful Native American look.

The female mask is done similarly, but the decoration is more delicate and the colors lighter. (See White Native American Mask and Black Native American Mask.)

St. Patrick's Day Couple

The couple that requested these masks would be attending a St. Patrick's Day parade and party in Chicago, Illinois. They didn't want to wear common things, but their costumes had to be green. I chose a green half mask for the man and cut a full green mask for the woman. They would be eating, drinking, and talking so they didn't want their mouths covered.

After coating the inside of each mask and pressing paper towels into them, I let them dry and cut the paper towel away from the eyeholes. I added a strip of foam over each eyehole of the woman's mask. Note that because the masks were now pliable, I could cut that interesting design into the lady's mask. I decorated the man's mask with green sequins, green glitter fabric paint, some lightweight green beads, and a green feather. But it needed something else. I chose a purple plastic fedora, coated it with Sculptural Arts Coating, and decorated it with green trim to match the mask.

I decorated the female mask with several shades of green feathers glued to the side, a green sequin applique in the middle, green sequin trim, and green glitter fabric paint. These masks should dress up any St. Patrick's Day party and still maintain a unique look. (See Man's Green Mask and Woman's Green Mask.)

Man's Green Mask

Woman's
Green Mask

Mardi Gras Couple

Mardi Gras colors are green, purple, and gold. Want masks for an elaborate couple that are easy to make? My smiling face and frown face were cut out of cardboard, coated with Sculptural Arts Coating, and covered with sequin trim and feathers. They are attached to dowel rods covered with sequin trim, maribu, and colorful wide tinsel. On the smiling face, I used green Christmas garland around the edge. These masks are lightweight, can be carried instead of worn, and they are Mardi Gras through and through. They make a great wall-hanging later. (See Happy Face Mask and Sad Face Mask.)

Jailbird Couple

The bird masks are two of my favorites. You've probably seen those plastic bird masks with a beak and a few yellow feathers stuck around them. They aren't much, but they have potential. These masks are not as cheap to make as the others because of the coque feathers used — coque feathers are harder to find and more expensive. Because these masks will be heavier, I would urge you to replace the thin elastic strap with a wider, sturdier piece.

Strip the sparse yellow feathers from the plastic masks. Coat the insides and press paper towels into them while they are still wet. After they are dry, trim off the edges of the towels. Before decorating

Happy Face Mask

Sad Face Mask

Jailbird Masks

Gold Half Mask

Flapper Mask

Unisex Elaborate
Mask

the fronts, remove the lenses from two pairs of plastic sunglasses and glue them over the eyeholes. Cover the outsides of the beaks with gold glitter fabric, the insides with red satin, and coat inside and out. Let dry. Decorate around the eyes with gold glitter fabric, rhinestones, and gold sequin trim. On the female, add big eyelashes. Trim the edges of the beaks in rhinestones. Use sewn together strips of coque feathers and glue them on — black on the male, white on the female. These masks were worn with prison outfits. (See Jailbird Masks.)

Plastic Half Masks

Plastic half masks come in all shapes, sizes, and colors. They are cheap to buy and easy to wear. And they are easy to decorate any way you want, from simple to elegant. Again, you need to be conscious of the weight of the trim used. If it's going to be too heavy, you must replace the thin elastic with wider, heavier elastic or Velcro.

I still coat these masks, even though I'm not going to cut them, to keep them more pliable and durable. However, if they are going to be used once and discarded, there is no need to coat them.

Basic Masks

I chose a slant-eyed **Gold Mask** for my first example. After trimming it with red sequins, I added drops of gold, black, and red fabric paint and finished it with lightweight gold beads, which I left hanging. (See Gold Half Mask.)

A small white half mask was transformed with a burst of green feather at the top, a white sequin applique, gold sequin trim, and fabric paint, topped off by some delicate gold beads hanging down the front. This would be a good mask to put with a roaring **Twenties Flapper.** (See Flapper Mask.)

A black half mask was the base for a very elaborate **Unisex Mask.** I glued a small round of poster board at the top to attach the feathers to, covered the mask with several colors of sequin trim, and framed the mask with black and silver maribu left hanging down each side. I glued a plastic star in the center of the feathers for the finishing touch. (See Unisex Elaborate Mask.)

As with the full white facemasks, the half mask can be glued to a stick for the person who wants a mask but doesn't want to wear it.

Jester Mask

This particular mask was made to accompany a jester costume. By gluing a piece of poster board with three curved tips to the top of the mask, I accomplished the look of a jester hat. I covered the poster board with sequin trim, edged it with black maribu, and added a sequin applique at each of the three tips.

After attaching the half mask to a dowel rod, I covered the rod with black maribu and decorated the mask with sequin trim. You would be amazed how little sequin trim it takes to design a half mask.

Remember, you can cut the wooden dowel rod to any length you desire. Attach the cut end to the mask to keep from catching a raw end on your costume. (See Jester Mask.)

Jester Mask

Foam Masks
Foam Animal Masks

Foam masks can be purchased in the same way and for the same cost as the full white faces and colored faces. You can buy groups of foam masks that are animals and others that are people. These are fantastic for productions in which children have to dress up as different animals or people. They work well if you're doing a float in a parade, or just for masquerade. Add them to a very simple costume and really dress it up.

I chose three animal masks to use as examples of what can be accomplished with very little work. You won't need to coat the inside of these; they are very soft. However, I normally coat the outside to help the glue adhere better.

Miss Pig Mask

Miss Pig was accomplished by gluing on eyelids made of pink felt covered with sequin trim and false eyelashes of black felt onto a pig mask. I added a black felt mole near the lip. Because I was going to use a blond curly wig with her, I clipped some curls off the wig and glued them around the face. The tiara is three gold leaf appliques glued to the top of the mask. Last, I added drop earrings and pink maribu to frame the face. (See Miss Pig Mask.)

Black Cat Mask

The Black Cat was made by gluing sequin trim onto a cat mask in spots and covering the mask with black maribu. The whiskers are lines of black fabric paint. (See Black Cat Mask.)

For the **Bunny,** I cut the ears off the rabbit mask and glued them onto a wide white headband. I used white sequin trim around the eyes, pink sequin trim on the nose and inside the ears, and covered the rest with white maribu. (See Bunny Mask.)

Bunny Mask

Calypso Woman
Mask

Elton John Mask

Foam People Masks

Foam people masks can be enhanced in the same way. Because you already have your basic structure, it's easy to look at the mask and decide what to do.

In particular, I liked the **Calypso Woman** mask. I know I could glitz it up with little effort. How colorful and fun she turned out! All I had to do was follow the design already on the face with sequin trim. I used a strip of fabric and Christmas beads to decorate the part of the hat nearest the face, covered the fruit with sequin trim, and added a green bow applique. Of course, adding feathers really dressed it up, and instead of earrings, I glued gold leaf appliques to each side of the mask. (See Calypso Woman Mask.)

We spoke of **Elton John** in the hats and headpieces section. One of the foam masks already had a pair of glasses built in. I used colored cellophane paper to cover the eyeholes, decorated around the glasses with sequin trim and appliques, and added a drop earring on one side. With the glitzy top hat, I think I caught the flavor of Elton John. (See Elton John Mask.)

All many people want is a hat and mask to wear with their clothes or a costume they come up with on their own. The foam masks are a wonderful addition and will dress up even a mundane costume. Creating the masks is a simple matter of adding a bit of trim as needed and a bit of imagination.

Chapter 7 Jewelry

Neckpieces

Adorning the neck has been common throughout the centuries. Today jewelry isn't as bold or as elaborate as in the past. It is easy to find jewelry second hand, and it doesn't matter if it is broken. We can still use it by making some simple modifications.

When one thinks of medieval jewelry, one usually thinks heavy and metal. Such jewelry would be hard to wear, but we can go for the look without the weight. When I was cutting a gray jumpsuit for a costume, I realized that the band at the waist would be a perfect start for my **Medieval Neckpiece.** I cut it out and cut the ends off to the desired length. I tacked Velcro on at the back for closure. By trimming the band with gold Christmas beads, I attained the metallic look. I finished it off with plastic jewels, gold buttons, and gold fabric paint. Because I left the beads hanging in the front, there was no need for a hanging necklace. (See Medieval Neckpiece.)

Medieval
Neckpiece

Victorian women wore high necklines and sought a more demure look. When making **Victorian** costumes, I often find a gown that's suitable, except it's not right at the neckline. Solving the problem is simply a matter of making something that gives the appearance of a high neckline. Find a blouse or another dress with the desired neckline. Cut out the neck and decorate it to match the gown. I found a rather straight white dress, one I couldn't use for a Victorian costume but that had that great high neck. I cut the neck out and glued some pink beaded fringe and a broach of pink flowers to it, and it gave the costume exactly what it needed. (See Victorian Neckpiece.)

Victorian Neckpiece

When making a **Mary Todd Lincoln** costume, I found a wonderful wedding dress and dyed it with black and purple dye to give it an antique look. The hat matched and was trimmed with black velvet. The dress cried out for something

Mary Todd Lincoln
Neckpiece

Naughty Lady
Neckpiece

Black Velvet
Necklace

Heavy Rhinestone
Showgirl Necklace

Light Rhinestone
Showgirl Necklace

special around the neck. By cutting the center out of a black velvet belt with gold ball closures in the front, I achieved the look I was going for. I finished it off by gluing a short cape made of the train of the wedding dress to the sides and back. It worked great and served a dual purpose. (See Mary Todd Lincoln Neckpiece.)

What about those wonderful naughty ladies from the past (i.e., the Miss Kitty, the victorian vamp, or the naughty belle who wants to turn heads)? If you are using a low-cut gown but want something outstanding at the neck, again you can cut the high neck out of a blouse or gown and decorate it to suit. This **Naughty Lady Neckpiece** was cut from a wedding dress I dyed black. I wanted a low-cut bodice. When cutting the dress, I left the zipper down, cut the neck out, and glued the edges under. Using the piece of ribbon that hangs the dress on a hanger, I made a tie in the back of the neckpiece. Because I wanted a vampier look, I glued black sequin trim to the edge and around the neck. I glued rhinestones from an old necklace to the neck and down the front, and placed a broach in the center. It worked well. (See Naughty Lady Neckpiece.)

There are times one is looking for a simpler look at the neck. By using a piece of wide, black velvet ribbon with a tie in the back, it can be easily accomplished. When making this **Velvet Neckpiece,** fold the ribbon into a V in front to give it a dressier look. If you are going to decorate the piece, glue a tie all the way around, leaving the ends long enough to tie a bow in the back. Cover the glued-on tie with fake jewels or an old necklace. (See Black Velvet Necklace.)

When creating a showgirl, one thinks of rhinestones. Watch for them. It's not that difficult to find old necklaces, rhinestones on purses, shoes, and clothing — occasionally even on hats. Wherever I see them for sale cheap, I buy them. Remember, it doesn't matter if the item is broken. To make a **Rhinestone Showgirl Necklace,** use a heavy felt in the desired color and make the necklace as wide or thin as desired. If it's to be a heavy necklace, use a tie for closure. Remember to run the tie around the whole piece, leaving enough in back to tie a bow. If the necklace is lighter weight, use a piece of Velcro to hold it in place. Glue rhinestones on. If you're using an old necklace, leave it hanging. (See Heavy Rhinestone Showgirl Necklace and Light Rhinestone Showgirl Necklace.)

One of the things you often find with high-necked gowns is that the zipper only goes to the bottom of the lace top, where it is split and has buttons at the neck. These are some of my favorite neckpieces to work with because you simply cut them out, trim them off, and decorate. You already have the closure at the back of the neck, so you save time several ways. While making a **Wine-Colored 1800s Gown,** I used this method. Because I wanted contrasting color, I removed a white applique and some white lace from the dress before I dyed it to glue to the neckpiece afterward. I think it gave the neckpiece a wonderful look with just a bit of trim and some pearls glued on. (See Wine and White Neckpiece.)

Wine and White
Neckpiece

Earrings and Bracelets

Earrings and bracelets can be accomplished using similar methods. The bracelet is made the same way as a showgirl necklace, and the earrings are made by taking a broken necklace, or pierced earrings with the backs broken off, and gluing them to a clip-on from another pair of earrings. When working with metal clips, it's better to glue a piece of felt over the clips before affixing the earrings to them. They will hold much better.

Women's adornment can be quite simple, but one must pay attention to the period of the gown or dress and accessorize appropriately. Long beads for the '20s, high necks for Victorian, heavy metal for medieval, and so on. The wrong jewelry can be as disastrous as the wrong hat.

Chapter 8

Collars, Cuffs, Flaps, and Capes

Egyptian Queen
Collar and Flap

Egyptian Queen

When my neighbor gave me an attractive blue evening dress with a low-cut neckline and split front, I thought of an Egyptian Queen. The only things needed to enhance it were a matching collar and front flap.

Making the Collar and Flap

1. Use a man's long-tailed shirt. Cut off the top half of the collar (the part that folds over), leaving the section with the top button intact.

2. Cut the top off the shirt, rounding from the top of the shoulders down to between the third and fourth buttons.

3. For the flap, cut out a section from the back of the shirt to the bottom of the long tail.

4. Turn the button on the shirt collar to the back for closure and cut off lower buttons. Turn the flap upside down.

5. Glue fabric on to cover both the flap and the collar. I chose gold with a scale design.

6. Glue the flap inside the sash belt.

7. Trim both the collar and the flap with gold sequin trim, adding gold rope trim, beads, and chains to the collar. Add gold fringe to the bottom of the flap.

T I P
Don't worry about hemming as long as you apply glue around the edge. The glue will seal it.

Pilgrim Man

I began my Pilgrim Man using a black frock coat (see how to make it in the jacket section). All that was needed to finish off the costume was a collar, cuffs, and a belt.

Pilgrim Collar and Cuffs

Making the Collar and Cuffs

1. Use a man's white shirt. Cut the top half of the collar off, leaving the top button intact.

2. Starting from beneath the top button, cut two squared off sections from the chest of the shirt, one on each side. Do the same in the back.

3. Cover the collar with a non-fray white fabric to give it a heavier look and glue matching seam binding around the edge for a finished look.

4. Cut the buttons off the cuffs of the sleeves. Glue the cuffs inside the jacket sleeves, leaving the white sleeve hanging down. Cut the sleeves off according to how big you want the cuffs. Turn the cuffs over on jacket sleeve.

5. After gluing their edges together, I covered the cuffs with the same fabric as the collar and trimmed them with seam binding.

T I P You don't have to cover the collar and cuffs. You can glue the edges under, but the look won't be quite as nice.

Man's Period Ruff

In the past, men and women wore high-necked, ruffled collars called ruffs. They were all different sizes, but usually white. If you're doing a period piece, don't complicate the ruff. It can range from simple to fancy, go right up to the chin, or lay around the neck.

Man's Period Ruff

Making the Ruff

1. Cut the collar and a small circle of fabric from a man's white shirt. Turn it backward so the top button will close in the back and the circle of fabric will hang down the front.

2. Trim the collar to the height you want the ruff.

3. Glue on some stiff, white ruffled trims — they don't all have to be the same — so they stand up. Touch glue onto the edge of the collar. Glue the rest laying down.

Snow White Collar

Neck Ruffle

String Tie

Ascot

Big-Bowed Tie

When making a **Large Stand-Up Collar,** think simple. There are a lot of blouses and dresses at the thrift shops with wide white collars. Buy one. I located mine attached to a very conservative, flowered dress. Because I intended to make a Snow White costume, all I had to do was glue the collar to the inside of the neckline, pull it tight on both sides to help it stand up, and glue it inside the vest bodice. It worked like a dream. (See Snow White Collar.)

A **Front Ruffle** for a period costume can be done one of two ways. Either cut the top of the collar off a man's white shirt — leaving the top button intact and a round section in the back — turn it backward, and glue on layers of ruffles to the round section, or attach a strip of fabric to another round piece of fabric layered in ruffled trim. (See Neck Ruffle.)

String Ties are difficult to find these days, but when doing an 1800s or Western production, they are necessary. If you can't find one, you can make one. You can still find narrow, black bow ties. Buy black ribbon and glue it to the bow tie so a piece hangs down on each side of center. Glue the edge of the ribbon under to keep from fraying. (See String Tie.)

I've used many things to make an **Ascot.** The one pictured here is a piece of silky fabric tied to a piece of elastic with Velcro attached to close it in the back. If you don't have a real tie tack, use an old earring or pin. It's the look you're going for after all, and this will work. (See Ascot.)

To make a **Big-Bowed Tie** for costumes such as the Wizard from *The Wizard of Oz,* make a small pillow from your fabric, pull it tight in the center and tie it with a piece of the same fabric, leaving the ends hanging down for that big tie look. Attach the bow to a piece of elastic to wear around the neck. Or, you could cut a bow off a gown and attach it to elastic. (See Big-Bowed Tie.)

I found an easy way to make a really fancy **Clown Collar** that stands up around the back of the head. First I removed the top of the collar from a man's red shirt, leaving the top button intact. I cut a large circle out of the top of the shirt. Because I save ruffles off a lot of the dresses I convert into costumes, I always have many in different colors and fabrics. I layered different colored ruffles to the shirt circle, beginning where the

Showgirl Clown Collar

buttons are in front of the shirt. I glued black maribu to the front, leaving it unglued where the button and buttonholes are. To make the collar stand up in back, I glued a child's pink tutu underneath the big collar. (See Showgirl Clown Collar.)

Like men's shirts, ladies' blouses and lightweight jackets can be used for collars. When making **Guenevere,** I needed a fancy white collar. I cut a circle out of the shoulders of a white brocade evening jacket with closure at the rounded neck. By enhancing it with gold trim, fake jewels, and fabric paint, I achieved the desired effect. To finish it, I glued a lightweight red cape made from the skirt of a prom dress to the underside of the collar. (See Guenevere Collar and Cape.)

For some costumes, such as **Cleopatra,** you might desire a sheer cape. I've found that lingerie works quite well. I cut a black nightie off under the arms, glued the cut edge to a piece of black seam binding, and glued it directly to the back of the collar in spots. The collar and cuffs are made from gold oilcloth with fake jewels glued on and fabric paint drops. The collar closes in the back with a tie. The cuffs simply fit over the arms. (See Cleopatra Collar, Cuffs, and Cape.)

I found an unusual tablecloth at a rummage sale for a dollar. It was oval with black satin on one side and a deep burgundy brocade on the other. I bought it and put it away for later use. At Halloween I needed a **Fancy Witch.** I pulled out the tablecloth, laid it on the floor long ways, and folded one end over a bit. I cut a slit along the folded edge for the neck and glued sequin trim around it to keep it from fraying. I glued burgundy trim on the inside edge and red trim on the outside. It hung beautifully. This type of cape would also work well for medieval costumes and could be done with a rectangular tablecloth. (See Witch Cape #1.)

One of the easiest capes is made from the skirt of a gown. It doesn't matter if the zipper is broken, because you won't need it. You can buy gowns with broken zippers much cheaper. When making a **Witch Cape,** I found a deep red dress with a long skirt and a broken zipper. It had a slight ruffle at the hem. I cut the

Guenevere Collar and Cape

Cleopatra Collar, Cuffs, and Cape

Witch Cape #1

Witch Cape #2

Viking Cape

skirt away from the bodice, turned it inside out, glued the waist shut, and added a black tie for the neck. I attached the cape to the wrists with ties on both sides. (See Witch Cape #2.)

Heavier capes are called for when making costumes for Viking, Cave Men, or Native American costumes. I find heavier robes make excellent capes. If you use a long robe and cut it off below the arms, it will be long enough. Close the cape with ties, Velcro, or perhaps a hook and eye. You can use the remaining fabric for belts, cuffs, or hair adornment as shown in the **Viking Cape** picture.

When creating **Columbus,** I found that the skirt from a prom dress glued to a long vest made of a robe achieved exactly the look I wanted. The difference between this cape and the others is that after the skirt is cut away from the bodice and the waist glued shut, the skirt is glued under the robe collar. (See Columbus Cape.)

A complete, grand costume can be made with a cape, a mask, and a hat. I was given this funny lady's mask with hair on it. I found the long black, satin cape — probably to be worn over an evening dress — at a thrift shop. I glued sequin trim around the edge of the cape and attached a hot pink feather boa with safety pins so it could be removed for washing. A decorated straw hat finished the **Funny Lady.** I wore it and it was an absolute hit. (See Funny Lady Cape Costume.)

Columbus Cape

Funny Lady Cape
Costume

Dolly Flaps

Dolly Flaps

"Hello Dolly — you're looking swell, Dolly," I said to myself when she was completed. The front of her dress, the glitzy part, was made from a long black skirt.

Making the Flaps

1. Begin with a skirt with an elastic waist. Cut a V out of the front of the skirt, leaving it attached to the elastic waist.

2. Cut a separate V out of the back of skirt.

3. Trim the edges of both V's with black fringe, then cover them completely by gluing on rows of red, black, and gold sequin trim.

4. Glue the V you cut from the back of the skirt directly to the bodice of the gown. Don't worry, it's washable.

5. Snip the elastic waist of the front V in the middle of the back and add a tie or Velcro for closure.

Chapter 9 # Wings

Butterfly Wings Front

Butterfly

I had a challenge. I needed a large set of butterfly wings for a Mardi Gras float. I tried using wire, but it didn't work well. The wings had to be lightweight, durable, and look as light as air. I hit on the idea of using boning from a hoop skirt. It was long enough, wider than wire so it was easier to work with, and covered with fabric so the glue would adhere well.

I found a sheer purple fabric with a subtle glitter design and used scraps of contrasting fabric in shades of purple, green, blue, and gold.

The upper wing is made from the largest hoop, and the lower wing is made from a smaller hoop glued to the larger hoop and bent into the shape of wings.

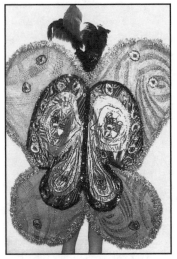

Butterfly Wings Back

Making the Wings

1. Remove the two largest hoops from the hoop skirt. Glue the ends of each hoop together to make two circles. Bend to the desired shape.

2. Lay the fabric out and cut around the wings twice, once for the front and once for the back.

3. Glue on contrasting fabrics where desired.

4. Glue gold garland around the edges.

5. Adorn with sequin trim.

6. Decorate a black back belt with black straps using black sequin trim and an applique to hide the front Velcro closure. I left beads hanging. Glue the wings directly to the back belt.

7. Using large safety pins and glue, attach the upper wing to the straps and cover where they're attached. Be sure to pinch the heads of the pins closed so there is no chance of them coming open.

(For the headpiece see the chapter on hats and headpieces.)

The costume can be worn over a black bodysuit or black leotard and tights, depending on how exposed one wants to be.

Any type of wing can be made easily with boning, but if you need **Smaller Wings,** I suggest you buy a set of packaged angel wings, bend them to the desired shape, and decorate. They can be spray painted and edged with everything from Christmas trim to sequin trim to feathers. (See Cupid Wings and Fairy Wings.)

Cupid Wings

Fairy Wings

Chapter 10 # Gloves, Belts, and Aprons

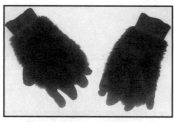

Brown Animal Gloves

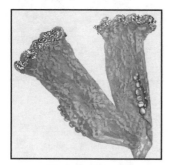

Glenda Gloves

Green and White
Lace Gloves

Movie Star Gloves

There is nothing worse than having your hands stuck in **Animal Paws.** It is nearly impossible to pick anything up. What if I told you there was an easy way to make animal hands that you could wear and still have the use of your fingers? Buy a pair of those one dollar, brown gloves you can get at the hardware store and glue a piece of brown fur over the back of them. This will give you that paw look with the freedom to use your fingers. For different animals, use different colored gloves and fur. (See Brown Animal Gloves.)

Long ladies' gloves are still pretty easy to find. If you can't get long gloves, check boutiques and wedding shops when they have a sale. If you are in a hurry and can't find gloves, or you desire the look of long gloves, but don't want to wear anything over your hands, try cutting the sleeves out of a gown and decorating them to match the costume you're making. After I dyed a wedding dress pink for **Glenda,** I cut the sleeves out. Then, when I needed a gloved look for the costume, I cut the sleeve to the desired length and glued silver sequin trim to the upper edge. (See Glenda Gloves.)

I made a **Mae West**-style gown of Kelly-green satin with white lace trim. No gloves! I cut the sleeves out of an old gown, glued green fabric and sequin trim to the raw edges, and added a green applique near the wrists. You'll find that by using glue at the top, the glove will stay up well. (See Green and White Lace Gloves.)

The gloves don't have to be lace. When making a dark purple velvet **Movie Star** gown, I wanted it sleeveless, so I cut the sleeves out and made them into gloves. The rhinestone buttons really set them off. (See Movie Star Gloves.)

I love to make belts. You can take a rather plain dress, add an unusual belt, and it makes all the difference. One day when I had to come up with a **Fairy** costume for a young woman, I hit on an idea. I bought a pink dress at the thrift shop. It had a sash tie sewn to each side. I cut a thin piece of cardboard into the shape I desired for my belt, then cut the sash ties off the dress and glued them together across the center the piece of cardboard. I glued felt on the other side of the cardboard and created a design using old sequin appliques and sequin trim to match the dress. (See Fairy Belt.)

Fairy Belt

This method continued to work for me as I made other costumes. I made a **Black Sequin-Covered Belt** that will work well for many costumes, i.e., a witch, a medieval woman, a wizard, even a sexy black cat or a showgirl. (See Black Sequin Belt.)

Black Sequin Belt

> **TIP**
> Any belt made with felt or cardboard will not be washable.

Fabric can also be used in creating these belts. When making a fancy **Black Cat** costume, I covered the cardboard with black satin fabric on both sides and decorated it with sequin trim and sequin and beaded appliques. I ran the tail, made from a black boa, through the sash tie in the back so it was doubled and not too long. Doubling the boa also made the tail look fuller. (See Black Cat Belt.)

Black Cat Belt

If you require an adjustable belt made of fabric, cut the fabric in the desired style and glue felt of the same color to the back. Tack Velcro on the outside of one end and the inside of the other, either in back or in front. The **Green Sequin Fabric Belt** closes in the front. I glued silver appliques and fake jewels on it. (See Green Sequin Belt.)

Green Sequin Belt

The purple and gold belt was made for an old **Dolly Parton** gown. It closes in the back. I used purple eyelash lamé and glued on gold sequin appliques. Remember, if you need gold or silver appliques, you can paint them with fabric paint. I cut all sorts of appliques off old gowns and paint them with gold leaf. (See Dolly Parton Belt.)

Dolly Parton Belt

Men's Belts are not all that difficult to find. Many times, one needs only to add a sash beneath them for a period look. If you need a more interesting belt, look in women's larger sizes. (See Viking Sash and Belt.)

Curtains can be answer for a **Colonial Apron.** You've seen those ruffled curtains that are short where they meet, then get longer and then short again. Making an apron out of them is

Viking Sash and Belt

Colonial Apron

Betsy Ross Apron

Pilgrim Apron

Man's Apron

simply a matter of gluing them into a white sash tie, taking tucks where needed. They hang perfectly for a colonial woman costume. (See Colonial Apron.)

Betsy Ross needed an apron for a parade costume. The costume also needed to be red, white, and blue. The gown was blue, the blouse and neckpiece were white, so I chose red and white striped fabric for the apron. I found a red and white striped cotton dress that buttoned down the front. I removed the buttons and cut the skirt off at the hem to the desired length. I turned the skirt backward. I cut a bib from the back of the dress and discarded the rest of the bodice. I glued the raw edges under and used Velcro to attach the top of the bib to the blue dress. I split the striped skirt up what is now the front to within an inch of the waist and glued the raw edges under. I glued the front and back corners of the skirt together on each side of the split and brought them up under the skirt. Then I glued them to the waist on each side to create that panier look. Turn the belt from the striped dress backward to finish the apron look. (See Betsy Ross Apron.)

A **Lady Pilgrim** isn't a pilgrim without her apron. I found an ankle-length white skirt, cut it to the desired length, and glued white piping to the bottom edge. The remainder of the skirt was used to make the cuffs and line inside the black and white bonnet. White dresses and skirts not only work well for aprons, but they also can be dyed and made into other costumes. Be sure to keep an eye out for them. (See Pilgrim Apron.)

If you happen to need a **Man's Apron** for one of Santa's elves, one of Snow White's dwarfs, or perhaps a cobbler, store clerk, or smithy, and you want real leather, buy an old coat and cut the apron out of the back. The ties at the neck and waist can be made by tacking on shoestrings. The same method will work with fabric, but you must use a non-fray fabric, hem it all the way around, or put a piping trim around the edge. (See Man's Apron.)

Because the '50s and '60s have always been a popular period for costumes, I have made a lot of carhops. The main accessories for the carhop are the hats and aprons. For the **Pink Carhop Apron,** I cut the waistband of a pair of checked pants off at the sides and tacked a pink sash tie from a dress to each side. I glued a small rounded piece of non-fray fabric to the inside of the waistband and decorated the edge with sequin trim. (See Pink Carhop Apron.)

For the **Black Carhop Apron,** I used the front of a skirt, tacked on a sash, and decorated it. (See Black Carhop Apron.)

Pink Carhop Apron

Black Carhop Apron

Chapter 11 Feet, Shoes, and Leggings

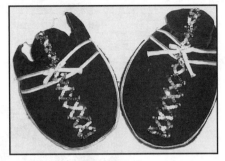

Clown Shoes

Clown Shoes

You might not think feet and shoes are that important, but to me, they are. After all, what would a clown be without big shoes or a rabbit without big feet? And speaking of clowns, my first example shows what you do when you have no clown shoes and are forced to make them.

Making the Shoes

1. Cut a piece of foam to form the top of the shoe as shown in the diagram.

2. Glue fabric to it, being sure to fold it under the edges.

3. Attach a piece of elastic or Velcro to the foam to fit around the back of the ankle.

4. Glue a piece of heavy fabric underneath the foam, from the toe to just in front of the heel, leaving it big enough for the front part of your shoe to fit inside.

5. Glue trim around the edge to cover where the foam is glued to the underside and decorate the shoe.

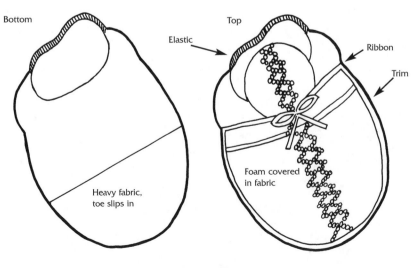

Clown Shoes

If you happen to be making a brown fur animal, you can use the same method to accomplish the look of **Animal Feet.** Simply cover the foam with fur instead of fabric. (See Bear Feet.)

Need some hooves for a **Unicorn?** Cover the foam with sequins and maribu. You could do other hoofed animals the same way by changing the fabric and trim. For instance, to make cow or horse hooves you might use a smaller piece of foam covered with a gray fabric and paint to make it shiny. (See Unicorn Feet and Lion King Feet.)

With some imagination, material, and trim, a pair of plastic clown shoes can make great animal and bird feet. They are the perfect size for **Rabbit Feet.** Cover them with fur, make a cuff at the top, glue it on, and use a heavier fabric underneath the toe. I close the cuff with Velcro and there are already holes for a tie at the ankle. Replace the tie with one the same color as your fur. (See Rabbit Feet.)

Bear Feet

Unicorn Feet

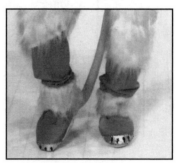
Lion King Feet

Rabbit Feet

Whoopi Goldbear House Shoes

Whoopi Goldbear House Shoes

When I had the occasion to make a costume called Whoopi Goldbear — designed like a costume from *Jumpin' Jack Flash* — clown shoes were the answer to those odd house shoes with penguins on the toes.

Making the Shoes

1. Buy two stuffed penguins, cut the bottoms off, and glue them to the plastic clown shoes.

2. Glue on long black fur to cover the shoes.

3. Glue a cuff of red fur to the ankles and add beads of fabric paint. I made matching hats and scarves for the penguins.

4. Make earmuffs of pink felt.

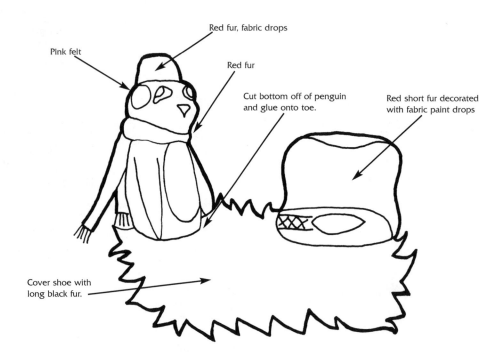

Red fur, fabric drops

Pink felt

Red fur

Cut bottom off of penguin and glue onto toe.

Red short fur decorated with fabric paint drops

Cover shoe with long black fur.

Whoopi Goldbear House Shoes

Jailbird Feet

The Jailbird Feet were built on a better pair of clown shoes. Actually, I found these at an auction. They were old and nearly worn out on top, but it didn't matter because I needed them for a base.

Jailbird Feet

Making the Shoes

1. Cut the toes from foam and cover them with gold glitzy fabric. The toenails are pieces of black felt covered with black fabric paint to make them shiny. Glue the toes on the clown shoes.

2. Cover the shoes with the same fabric as the toes, being sure you leave the area around the laces open.

3. Glue maribu under the toes and coque feathers around the shoes at the ankles.

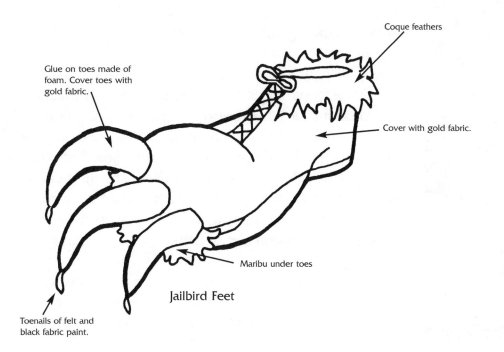

Glue on toes made of foam. Cover toes with gold fabric.

Coque feathers

Cover with gold fabric.

Maribu under toes

Toenails of felt and black fabric paint.

Jailbird Feet

Yellow Chicken Feet

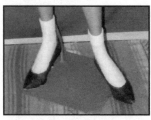

Dorothy Shoes

Queen of Siam Shoes

Buckle Shoes

Men's Spats

Women's Spats

There is another type of clown shoe that is made similarly to my foam feet and shoes. It is rounded and hooks around the back of the ankle. Again, these are quite useful in making animal and bird feet, although they are not as cheap as the foam shoes. My example is a pair of **Yellow Chicken Feet** made over the clown shoes. The toes are foam covered with orange sequins, and the feet are covered with long yellow fur. The closure is already built in so you don't have to worry about that. (See Yellow Chicken Feet.)

Some regular shoes are adaptable but only if they are going to be used for one specific person. They are simple to convert and still give you the desired look. When I did a production of *The Wizard of Oz*, **Dorothy** needed those famous red shoes. I covered a pair of my player's shoes with red glitter fabric paint. Fabric paint works well if the shoe is made of fabric. If the shoes are made of patent leather or any slick fabric, you'd be better off to glue sequin trim on. (See Dorothy Shoes.)

Over the years, those little stretchy shoes have been great for a number of costumes. When I did the **Queen of Siam** and needed the turned-up-toe shoes, I began with a pair of gold, glitzy stretch shoes. By cutting a triangle of fabric, gluing the edges together, stuffing it with fiberfill, then gluing it on the toe of the shoe, I got exactly the look I was going for. I finished the decoration with drops of fabric paint and a jewel on the end of each toe. You can use this same method on a boat shoe for a male. Paint the boat shoe with glitter fabric paint. (See Queen of Siam Shoes.)

Sometimes a decoration as simple as a buckle can change a new shoe into a **Period Shoe.** I use this process on a lot of men's shoes to make period costumes. The buckle is made from four pieces of decorated felt and glued on. (See Buckle Shoes.)

It's certainly not an easy prospect to find **Spats** these days, unless you buy them at a costume shop or through a costume company. If you happen to be doing a production like *Guys and Dolls* and need a number of pairs of spats, it can get expensive. Or maybe not. The solution is socks! Yes, I make my spats from socks. They come in all sizes and colors today, are stretchy, and are easy to covert. They can be slipped over women's or men's shoes, even over boot shoes. (See Men's Spats and Women's Spats.)

Sleeves from robes make great leggings. Say you need leggings for your **Prince** costume. Princes wore those ones with the pointed toes. Don't use a fitted sleeve; you'll want it full. Cut the sleeve off at the shoulder and turn it upside down. The part that attaches to the shoulder will become the foot. Glue the rounded shoulder part under enough to fit over the toe of the shoe, leaving it with a point. Tack a piece of elastic just in front of the heel and another piece inside the top of the legging so it goes not quite halfway around. That prevents the legging from slipping down. Wear socks underneath. (See Prince Leggings.)

When using a fur robe to make leggings, cut the sleeve out and square it off. Wrap the sleeve around the ankle and lace a strip of contrasting fur or fabric around it to hold it up. These are good for **Vikings, Cave Men,** and even some **Native American** costumes. (See Viking Leggings.)

Using the sleeves from a brown fur robe, some foam, and a bit of the fur from the remaining robe, I made **Animal Legs and Feet.** These were needed to go under the mother's dress in the Three Bears. The only thing I did differently here was to fold the fur over at the top and then add a drawstring to help hold the legging up. The feet are made like the foam clown shoes and covered with fur from the robe. They are glued to the end of the sleeves. (See Animal Feet and Legs.)

When I made a **Warrior Princess** costume, I needed something for the legs. I coated a pair of plastic armor leggings with Sculptural Arts Coating, covered them with black velvet sleeves from an old dress and decorated them with silver fabric and silver sequins. I replaced the ties in the back with black shoestrings. The girl who needed the costume wore black shoes and the look worked for the purpose.

Boot Tops can be made from the sleeves of a soft leather coat (see legging examples) by cutting the legs out of a pair of leather or vinyl pants, or you can make them from scratch. Remember to use a soft leather or faux leather, making the tube larger at the top than the bottom and a shaping piece to go over the front of the shoe. (See Boot Tops.)

Prince Leggings

Viking Leggings

Animal Feet
and Legs

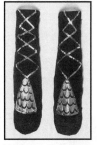

Warrior Princess
Leggings

Boot Tops

Chapter 12 Undergarments

Don't make undergarments a bigger problem than they are. Remember, they usually will be hidden under the outer garment. Even if they must show, there are ways of making them that will give the illusion of authenticity.

Pantaloons, for instance, usually show at the bottom. So all you need to do is cut a pair of woman's white stretch pants to the desired length and glue rows of ruffles to the legs.

PVC Hoop Skirt

If you're lucky, you can find hoop skirts in thrift shops that carry wedding and prom dresses. If not, see the reference section to find out where to buy them. If you're in a hurry and don't have time to look or order, go to the hardware store.

Making the Skirt

1. Decide how big your hoops should be by measuring the skirt you're going to put the hoops under at the hips, knees, and ankles. Buy three sections of plastic PVC tubing in corresponding lengths. Connect the ends or each tube with duct tape to form a circle.

2. To make the waist of the hoop skirt, use a wide piece of elastic that fits the waist of the overskirt, or use a belt.

3. Connect the smallest hoop to the elastic waist or belt, allowing it to stand out at the hip. I use seam binding tape. Connect the middle hoop to the smallest hoop the same way, and the largest at the bottom.

4. If you need the underskirting to show at the bottom of the skirt, glue a wide ruffle to the bottom hoop.

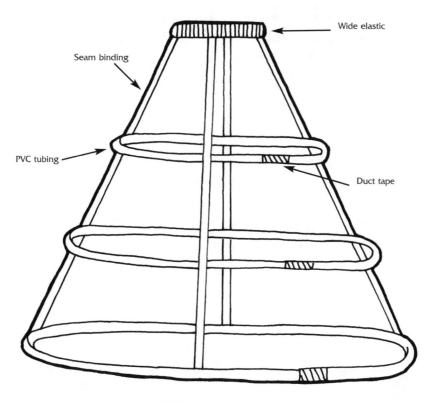

PVC Hoop Skirt

Farthingales

I like working with hoop skirts because they are versatile garments. When attempting to create a Queen Isabella or a Queen Elizabeth, you must consider the **Sixteenth-Century Farthingale.** You won't find one of those in a thrift shop, but you can covert a hoop skirt or PVC tubing into one.

With the farthingale, you must consider the weight of the garment you're wearing over it. Are you using velvet or polished cotton? There's a big difference. If you are using a lightweight fabric, even on the side panels, the hoop skirt works great one of two ways. If you want your skirt to stand out only on the sides, remove the boning from a hoop skirt. Locate a dress or pants with a waistband with belt loops. Cut the waistband off the skirt, leaving an inch to glue under. Run the boning through the loops of a waistband. Use several large safety pins to hold the ends of the boning together. Pinch the

Farthingale #1

Circle Farthingale

heads of the safety pins. This will not only keep the ends of the boning secured, but will allow you to slide the boning for size adjustment. (See Farthingale #1.)

If you need the **Circle Farthingale,** pull the waist of the hoop skirt above the chest, tie it in at the waist. Bring the bottom hoop up to the middle hoop and attach in spots with large safety pins. Pinch the heads to keep them from coming open. If you like this method better and need the farthingale that only stands out on the sides, fasten a piece of elastic to each side of the hoop in the front and back and pull the hoop together. (See Circle Farthingale.)

When using heavier garments for the skirting, use PVC tubing. It will hold out wonderfully, but still be lightweight and easy to wear.

> **T I P** You can make the skirt for a farthingale costume easily by sewing several skirts together. Use the heavier fabric in front and back and lighter fabric on the sides.

Bustles

Bustles can be made from many items. Once, in a pinch, I made a **Back Bustle** from a round, plastic vegetable colander. If you want **Side Bustles,** hook a couple of lightweight pillows to a piece of elastic that fits the waist. For a back bustle, the same method will work. Since many of the gowns from that period are layered, you can even pin and glue your pillow between the layers as long as it is washable. Pillows, balled up netting, small plastic bowls, and rolled up foam will work, depending on the type of gown. Just make sure it is hidden.

If you need a full flow to the floor in the back, make your bustle, then attach netting — you might retrieve some from an old wedding or prom dress — double it over several times and hook it to the bustle. It will give you that wonderful stand out clear to the hem. With bustles, use whatever works.

Cancans and Petticoats

You don't want to make a cancan or petticoat from scratch. It's expensive, time consuming, and an exercise in frustration. There are easier ways. Watch for rummage sales that advertise square dancing clothes. Sometimes, if they aren't too expensive, you can find great cancans there.

If you can't find one and you need to make one, look for dresses that have a lot of netting underneath. Cut the skirt away from the bodice at the waist, leaving the netting intact, and turn it wrong side out. Remove the zipper, and glue the waist and the edges where you removed the zipper under. Attach half a shoestring to each side so it can be tied to fit. You not only have your cancan or petticoat, depending on the length, but the skirting next to your skin will keep it from scratching.

Corsets, Busts, and Bras

While you're rummaging, look for unusual undergarments. I found a really big-boned corset with full bra. It was easily converted to make a thin woman or man look like a **Full-Figured Woman** by stuffing the bra cups with fiberfill, gluing felt over the back, and adding two pillows in the back for a more rounded look. Because the corset hooked on the side, it was perfect. (See Padded Corset Bra.)

Padded Corset Bra

Speaking of busts, you can make one out of those foam footballs, cut in half and glued to elastic. The look will surprise you.

However you make your undergarments, keep in mind the word *under.* Unless it is seen, it doesn't matter how it's made as long as it is easy to wear and creates the look you want.

Costumes from Bras, Corsets, and Rib Belts

Strapless Belly Dancer

For the woman who wants a really skimpy top to go with a **Belly Dancer** costume, a black strapless bra will work. By gluing on fake jewels, adding silver fabric paint around them and some silver trim, a belly dancer top is born. (See Strapless Belly Dancer.)

Purple Belly Dancer Bra

For the more **Full-Figured Belly Dancer** who requires straps, a full, padded bra should be used. You'll want padding because it holds up better when gluing trim on. After finding a dress with purple, black, white, and gold in the sheer skirt, I used the fabric from the bodice to cover the bra. After gluing on the purple fabric, I trimmed the bra with gold, purple, and black sequin trim and lightweight purple beads left hanging down in front. I added a piece of gold, glitzy fringe to each shoulder. Because there was white in the skirt, I used a white bra. Use a color that matches because the stretchy part of the bra around the side and back will show. (See Purple Belly Dancer Bra.)

Purple Belly Dancer Skirt

A rib belt is a stretchy, fabric belt that fits around the rib cage after someone has broken his or her ribs. They can be purchased in medical supply stores and pharmacies, and they are not very expensive. They come in many different sizes. You'll need to find one that fits around the hip without stretching. They are made with a heavy Velcro closure. When doing a Belly Dancer Skirt, the belt will close in the front.

Purple Belly
Dancer Skirt

Making the Skirt

1. Lay rib belt out flat. Cut the skirt off the dress and glue it to the bottom outside of the rib belt, making sure not to cover the Velcro.

2. Glue some fabric over the belt, again making sure not to cover the Velcro.

3. Spot glue beads and leave them hanging in loops.

4. Decorate the belt using sequin trim and fringe.

5. When you close the belt, it will overlap to cover the Velcro.

Gold and Black Belly
Dancer Skirt

The **Gold and Black Belly Dancer Skirt** was made by using the skirt of a sheer black nightie, cut off under the arms. I glued the skirt onto a rib belt, hung lined rhinestones around the skirt, and attached gold sequin trim and appliques. To ensure full coverage, I layered the belt with black trim lined with black discs. Because I didn't cover this belt with fabric, I dyed it black first. The belts take dye quite well. (See Gold and Black Belly Dancer Skirt.)

Feathered Showgirl Rib Belt

Rib belts can make the job of costuming showgirls so easy. If you want feathers in the back, either hanging or standing up, and have some feather boas and a rib belt, you are almost there. Unlike the belly dancer, who needs the rib belt to fit around the hip, you'll need one that fits the waist. Remember, once you use glue on it, it will no longer stretch. The front Velcro closure enables you to do whatever you need in the back.

Feathered Showgirl
Rib Belt

Making the Belt

1. Lay the rib belt out flat. Glue strings of tiny black beads around the bottom edge.

2. Make two splits in the back of the belt. Weave a piece of flat spring wire through them, leaving plenty to hang off the back.

3. Glue gold fabric to cover the entire belt, except at one end where the ends overlap to close in the front.

4. Trim with gold sequin trim and gold fringe.

5. Glue sheer gold netting to the back of belt.

6. Glue one and a half black feathers boas to the spring wire. Glue the other half to a strapless black satin bustier.

7. Glue a piece of foam and felt over the spring wire inside the belt so the metal never touches the wearer.

8. Complete the costume with a pair of black exercise briefs and a headpiece.

It's quite easy to find all types of lingerie at garage sales and thrift shops. Look for the boned bustiers to turn into corsets and tops. You can take a really plain-looking dress and turn it into something special by adding a corset. Because I make a lot of dance hall costumes and medieval costumes, this easy corset has served me well.

The first corset started out a bustier. I cut it off just below the cups and secured the boning by shooting some glue in and pinching the fabric together. If the boning goes higher than you wish, bend it over and pinch it flat with pliers instead of trying to cut it off. Any place that doesn't need to stretch, which is the front,

Black and Purple
Corset

Medieval Corset

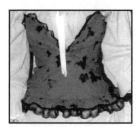

Colonial Tavern
Wench Corset

Dance Hall Bodice

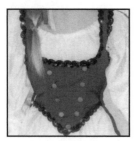

German Corset

can be decorated with beading, sequin trim, and fringe if desired. This **Black and Purple Corset** was made to go over a dance hall dress. (See Black and Purple Corset.)

The next bustier was a half-cup one that didn't need to be cut. It was perfect to go over my **Medieval Gown.** I accentuated the cups by gluing silver and green sequin trim on them and making a metallic look with drops of silver fabric paint. I decorated down the body with drops of green and silver fabric paint and a double line of silver sequins in the center. I attached a silver chain to the bottom to hang down the front of the dress and trimmed the edge with silver sequins. This corset just made the gown. (See Medieval Corset.)

Strapless dresses are useful in making tops and corsets for period costumes. The shape is there, the boning is there, so all you have to do is add some imagination and trim.

When making a **Colonial Tavern Wench,** I found a flowered dress with boning in the bodice. I dyed it red, cut the skirt away, and cut the bodice into a deep V that didn't affect the boning. I left just a bit of the skirt at the bottom for a flouncy look. I removed the back zipper and tacked in hooks and eyes and trimmed with black lace. (See Colonial Tavern Wench Corset.)

I cut the skirt off a black strapless gown with a fitted skirt so I could make a top for a **Dance Hall Costume.** Because the back was made of stretch fabric, I didn't have to worry about zippers. I glued colorful sequin trim and maribu onto the front. It would be worn with a flared black skirt and cancan. (See Dance Hall Bodice.)

I needed a front, jumper-looking corset for a **German Costume** for Oktoberfest. By using a jumpsuit dyed with red and brown dye, I came up with my corset. The jumpsuit closed in the front, so it was perfect. I cut the pants away and cut the bodice down to where the buttons were. After that, I glued bronze sequin trim around the edges and the corset was ready to go. For this particular costume, boning was not needed. (See German Corset.)

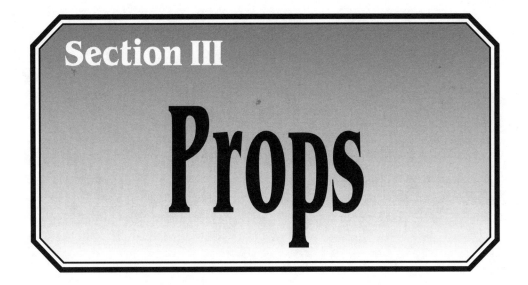

Section III

Props

Chapter 13 Native American Props

It is absolutely wonderful if you can find suede cloth or doe hide to use for Native American props, but it isn't always possible. I've run into problems finding it, so I've had to improvise.

I have found that a thin brown, beige, or tan robe works well. It's a non-fray fabric, it fringes great, and it gives the illusion of suede cloth.

For the **Male Native American Headband,** I used a strip of brown fabric, glued four feathers together, wrapped the quills with fabric — which I left hanging down in strips — and glued the strip to the inside of the headband. The band ties in back. You can't get much simpler than that.

The **Female Native American Headband** is a bit wider than the male's and is decorated with drops of fabric paint to make it look beaded. I chose to leave the feathers hanging down. They are glued inside the band. The band ties in back. You'll notice that on the yoke of the robe I used for the costume, I used the same design and colors as the headband. The neckpiece is nothing more than three pieces of fabric, braided and decorated. It ties in the back.

Male Native American Headband

Female Native American Headband

Scabbard

The male Native American was a hunter. In the early years, the hunters used bows and arrows. To make the Scabbard and Bow, I chose two brown robes, one dark and one tan.

Scabbard and Bow

Making the Prop

1. Fold over one side of the tan robe to form a rectangle and leave enough fabric to make fringe. Glue the bottom and sides of the rectangle to form the scabbard. Fringe excess fabric.

2. Glue on some dark brown robe material in four places.

3. If you want a leather look, coat the scabbard with Sculptural Arts Coating. It will hold the fabric stiff.

4. Add beading with drops of fabric paint. The beading will cover where you glued the scabbard together.

5. Make the strap from three strips of tan robe, braided and glued to the scabbard. I secured the hold with safety pins, pinched the heads to keep them closed, and covered them with trim.

6. I glued some extra strips of fabric to the bottom corner and glued a couple of feathers and maribu on just for the look.

7. The arrows are wooden dowel rods with the ends of feathers glued on.

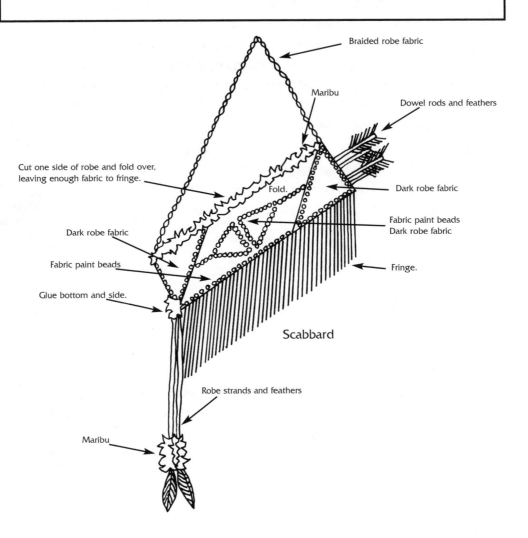

Bow

Making the Prop

1. Punch two holes in each end of a black, plastic stick from an old devil trident. I used a nail.

2. Run line from a weed whacker through the holes at one end, pull it several inches down, and secure it to the stick with duct tape.

3. Push the line through the holes at the other end, pull until the pole is bent, and secure the line the same way.

4. Cover the stick with tan and brown strips of robe fabric.

5. Add some beading with fabric paint, glue on strands with feathers, and decorate with brown maribu.

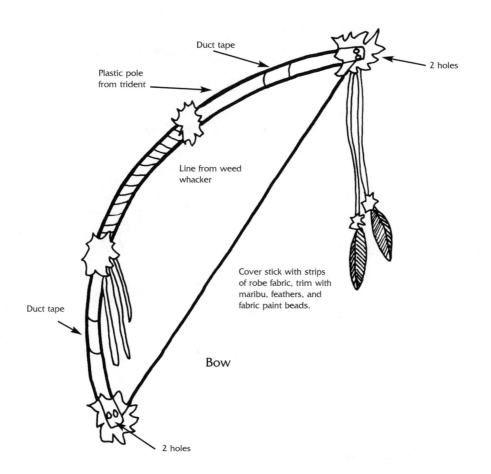

Duct tape

Plastic pole from trident

2 holes

Line from weed whacker

Cover stick with strips of robe fabric, trim with maribu, feathers, and fabric paint beads.

Duct tape

Bow

2 holes

Rifle Scabbard

Rifle Scabbard

Later, Native American males used rifles. Because they hunted on horseback and on foot, they had to have a way to carry their guns.

I used the same tan robe I had used for the bow and scabbard to make the rifle scabbard.

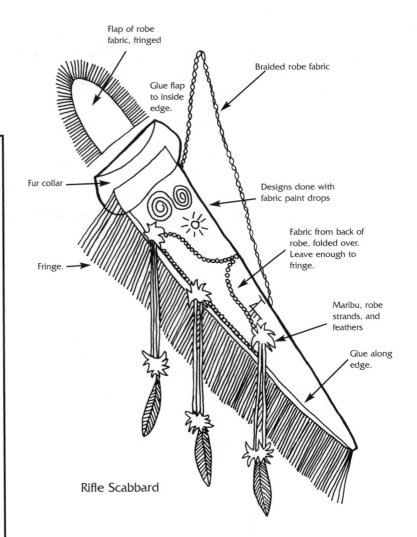

Rifle Scabbard

Making the Prop

1. Using the back of the robe, fold the fabric over to form a long triangle, leaving enough excess to make fringe.

2. Glue down the side across from the fold and along the bottom.

3. Fringe excess fabric.

4. Cut three long strips of fabric, braid them, and affix them to the scabbard with pins and glue.

5. I made petroglyph designs with drops of fabric paint. All beaded trim is drops of fabric paint.

6. Glue a fur collar from a coat around the opening.

7. Glue the piece of fabric that would hang over the butt of the gun inside the opening and decorate it.

8. Glue on some longer fringe in three spots along the bottom of the scabbard. Glue on feathers and maribu for decoration.

Seed Pouch

For the Native American female, I made a pouch to carry seeds instead of scabbards, bows, and arrows. Using fabric from the brown robe, I cut out two identical U's, leaving enough excess around them to fringe.

Seed Pouch

Making the Prop

1. Cut two pieces of fabric into identical U's. Leave extra on the bottoms and sides to fringe. Glue pieces together, leaving the top open.

2. Cut fringe.

3. Glue a separate piece of fabric inside the back of the opening, leaving it long enough to hang over.

4. Decorate with fabric paint drops to look like beading.

5. Glue some feathers and real beads to the fringe.

6. Braid three strips of fabric and glue them beneath the flap at the opening.

Chapter 14 Wands and Poles

Jester Pole

Wizard Pole

When moving to Arizona, friends gave us a set of walking poles made of aluminum with wooden handles and a loop at the top. Because my husband and I are short, the walking poles were too tall for us. I put them away in a corner of my house for several years. One day when I needed to make a Jester Pole and Wizard Pole, they came to mind.

For the **Jester Pole,** I applied Sculptural Arts Coating to a cheap purple plastic mask. I lined the inside with green felt so it showed through the mouth and eyeholes. I attached the mask directly to the handle of the walking pole, gluing green felt to the edge of the mask and around the pole. Once I thought it was secure, I decorated it. Starting at the bottom, I wrapped colorful sequin trim around the pole to cover it. I decorated the mask with gold trim and sequin appliques and red fabric paint on the lips. For the finishing touches, I glued feathers to cover the back, white maribu around the face, and strips of sequin trim and beads to hang down. The pole, with the mask, is fifty-eight inches tall. (See Jester Pole.)

The **Wizard Pole** is made the same way, with one significant difference. Instead of a mask, I used a devil's claw, which is a ball of dried, intertwined desert vine. They are easy to find in Arizona, but if you can't find one where you are, you can use almost any kind of ball. I sat the ball on top of the pole and ran a piece of wire through the hole in the handle where the loop had been. Then I wrapped the wire around the ball. I spray painted the devil's claw with gold spray paint, worked some glitter pipe cleaners in and out of it, added some long strings of fabric, yarn, beads and sequins, and a touch of maribu where the ball meets the pole. The pole is approximately sixty inches tall. (See Wizard Pole.)

When I had an occasion to make a **Zulu Costume,** I needed a pole for a prop. I bought an extension feather duster at a rummage sale for two dollars. It had great natural-colored feathers on top. With the pole completely extended (which made it quite tall) I glued strips of colorful fabric around it in sections. I tied contrasting pieces of fabric to each section, leaving some hanging down, then glued feathers and dried chicken bones and beads to them. It was a realistic addition to my Zulu man. (See Zulu Pole.)

Wands are very easy to make. If you can't find one to buy, simply use a wooden dowel rod, stick something on the end — perhaps a heart, a star, or a circle — and decorate. **Glenda's Wand** was made from a dowel rod, cut shorter and covered with pink sequins. The end is foam covered with sequins. The **Queen of Hearts Wand** was a purchased wand to which I added a red heart decorated with sequins. (See Glenda Wand and Queen of Hearts Wand.)

Zulu Pole

Queen of Hearts Wand

Glenda Wand

Chapter 15 Armor

Plastic Armor Original

Throughout my early costuming years, armor remained a problem to make. I tried several methods, but was never completely happy with the results. Then I discovered cheap, plastic armor. It wasn't bad looking the way it was, but it didn't last. Because it was plastic, it had a tendency to break and crack.

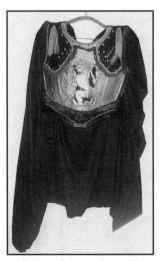

Armor Breastplate #1

Armor Breastplate #1

The plastic armor breastplate was made in two sections that connected at the shoulders with Velcro and under the arms with ties. Later, they made the underarm connections with Velcro. It still wasn't what I wanted.

I kept looking at it. The form was there and the decoration wasn't bad, if only I could make it look better and last longer. When I discovered Sculptural Arts Coating, it was the answer to my problem. As I looked at the plastic armor again, I realized I could make two breastplates out of one set of plastic armor. With some ingenuity, it worked.

Making the Armor

1. Coat the inside of the plastic breastplate with Sculptural Arts Coating. Let dry and spray paint.

2. Coat the center front with Sculptural Arts Coating and press fabric into it. Spread a coat over the fabric, leaving the design in the center area uncoated. Let dry and cut out around the design.

3. Add black dye to the coating and paint the shoulders and the lip at the bottom. I also used some black coating around the lion on the front to give it definition.

4. Using gold leaf paint, cover the fabric and the lion. Let dry.

5. Decorate with strips of fur along the outer edge and gold Christmas beads.

6. Use gold leaf paint to make rivets. Sweep some over the fur edging to give it a more interesting look.

7. Staple Velcro to the shoulders and under the arms of the breastplate to attach the backpiece and cape.

8. Make a pillow of foam covered with fabric and attach it to the shoulders with Velcro. It will hang off the back and give the look of a back piece. The cape was the skirt off a black dress. Add Velcro where appropriate so it hangs the way you want it. The cape will hang over the pillow to hide it.

9. Add gold tassels at the shoulder to cover the Velcro.

The **Back of the Breastplate** is enhanced in much the same way, but because there is no design on it, I created my own design using some blue applique I'd taken off a dress. I used gold leaf paint on the front and the appliques at the shoulders. With the wonderful gold leaf paint that I buy from our local hardware store, it doesn't matter what it is — I can make it gold. (See Breastplate #2.)

Breastplate #2

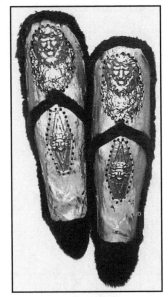

Armor Leggings

Leggings for armor can be accomplished using the same method as for the breastplates. It doesn't really matter what fabric you use to cover the area you want to coat and paint, as long as you use the same on all the parts of the armor. Be sure to not sculpt or coat over the areas you wish to cut out, or the fabric will stick. On the leggings, I cut out two sections. I trimmed the leggings with strips of black fur and some black fabric paint drops. Because the original ties in the back were made of thin white fabric, I replaced them with round black bootlaces. If the coating gets over the holes, use a sharp sturdy object to punch it out. (See Armor Leggings.)

Helmet

When my helmet arrived, it was even thinner plastic than the armor. What to do? I really didn't want to cover it with fabric — too tacky. Fortunately, I still had some appliques off a dress. I did use some fabric on the very back of the helmet.

Helmet Front

Helmet Side

Making the Armor

1. Coat the inside of the helmet with Sculptural Arts Coating. Let dry and spray paint gold.

2. Coat the outside and press fabric into the part that hangs down in the back. Coat over the fabric. Let dry.

3. Glue appliques on and paint them with gold leaf.

4. Glue a section of a black feather boa to the top and back. Trim off all the feather ends that stand out.

5. Punch the holes on the side open and use a thin black shoestring as a tie.

**T
I
P**
If you need more design in empty spots, add it with glue from a glue gun and gold leaf over it.

No suit of armor is complete without a shield and sword. I coated the **Shield** with Sculptural Arts Coating on both sides. I added some pieces of black fabric and coated over them. Everything else was gold leafed. For the outer trim, I used black maribu. Another option would be to use a strip of black fur. (See Shield.)

I bought a cheap, plastic **Sword and Sheath** and a black belt with a big, gold buckle. I gold leafed the sword handle and painted the blade with chrome. I decorated the handle with a gold broach that looked Celtic and used some gold fabric paint on the blade. The sheath is gold leafed with a leather bootlace glued around it and black, plastic discs glued where the lace crosses. I attached the sheath to a black belt with gold studs made from fabric paint. (See Sword and Sheath.)

Shield

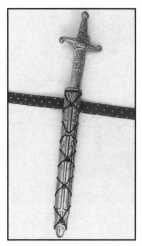

Sword and Sheath

Chapter 16
Thrones, Crowns, and Scepters

King's Throne

King's Throne

I like to use wooden ladder-back chairs to make thrones. They work well because as I build the throne, I can weave through the ladder back. I can also attach fabric to the back to show through and add color. When searching for the right chair, consider the shape. For the King's Throne, I chose a rocking chair and removed the rockers. It was the perfect shape except for the rockers. It had wide, rounded arms and the ladder back had holes wide enough to really show off the fabric. For the cushion, find a pillow that covers the seat and extends over the sides a bit.

King's Throne
Original Chair

Making the Throne

1. If you're using an old chair, wash it off and let it dry completely. The less finish it has on it, the better.

2. To make the back taller and the arms wider, cut a child's foam swim tube in half lengthwise, and then cut one half in half again lengthwise so you have two long quarter pieces. I use an electric knife to cut the tube.

3. Weave the uncut half from the bottom of the ladder to above the top of the ladder back, leaving an arch at the top.

4. Cut one of the quarter lengths of swim tube in half crosswise to make two shorter pieces. Set the long quarter piece aside. Glue the two short quarter tubes to the outside of the arms.

5. Glue large spools to the arms and back poles. I used empty ribbon spools made of cardboard and plastic.

6. Using rope of your choice, trim the foam and the tops of ladders.

7. Glue on whatever decoration you wish. I used Christmas beads, old necklaces I took apart, and some balls I removed from a hat. Glue on where desired. It doesn't make any difference what color things are. Coat the entire surface and decoration with Sculptural Arts Coating and let dry.

8. Spray paint the whole thing with gold.

9. Put the pillow on the seat, fold it over the sides, and staple it to the bottom of the chair on both sides. Don't pull it too tight, or the staples could pull out when someone sits on it.

10. Choose some appropriate fabric. I chose a heavy, dark purple satin. Glue the fabric to the back, behind the foam loop and the holes between the ladders. Glue fabric under the seat to cover the edges of the pillow.

11. Using Dalmatian fur — white with black spots — cover where you glue the trim on in the back. I glued the same fur on the front to decorate it and give it that finished look.

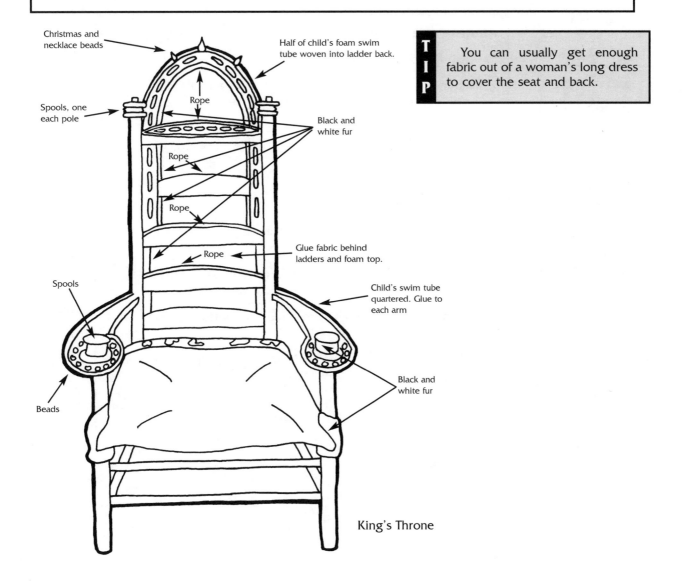

Christmas and necklace beads

Half of child's foam swim tube woven into ladder back.

Rope

Spools, one each pole

Black and white fur

Rope

Rope

Rope

Glue fabric behind ladders and foam top.

Child's swim tube quartered. Glue to each arm

Spools

Beads

Black and white fur

King's Throne

T I P You can usually get enough fabric out of a woman's long dress to cover the seat and back.

Queen's Throne

Queen's Throne
Original Chair

Queen's Throne

When building a Queen's Throne, think more delicate, more decorative lines, and either thin arms or no arms. I prefer the look with no arms. I used a straight-backed, armless, ladder-back chair. It had curves in the ladder back and interesting knobs on the side poles. Because I'd cut one quarter piece of the child's foam swim tube in half to make the arms for the King's Throne, I still had one long quarter left.

Making the Costume

1. Wash the chair and let it dry.

2. Weave the quarter of the child's foam swim tube from the inside of the bottom ladder to the top, leaving an arch at the top.

3. Decorate the chair with rope, twine, beaded trim, and Christmas beads. Coat the entire structure with Sculptural Arts Coating and let dry.

4. Spray paint with gold paint. Let dry.

5. Fold the pillow over the edges and staple it under the chair on both sides — not too tight.

6. Glue pieces of fabric to the holes from the back. I used scraps of red velvet. Glue trim over the edges.

7. Glue fabric under the chair to cover the bottom of the seat. I used red satin.

8. I had some red satin buttons from the dress I used to cover the chair, so I glued them to the foam and three of the ladders.

9. Glue gold fringe around the seat and the bottoms of the poles.

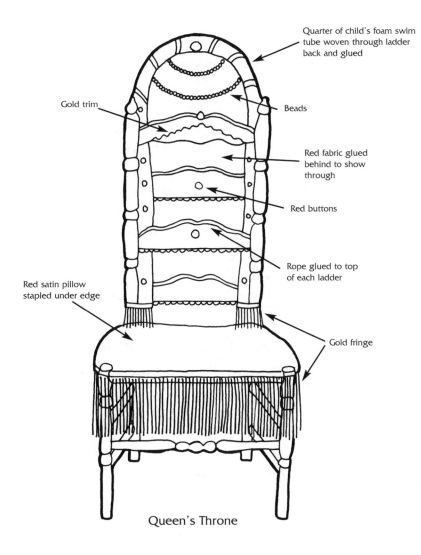

Quarter of child's foam swim tube woven through ladder back and glued

Beads

Gold trim

Red fabric glued behind to show through

Red buttons

Rope glued to top of each ladder

Red satin pillow stapled under edge

Gold fringe

Queen's Throne

Because all the items used for the thrones were from second-hand stuff, they were very inexpensive to make, and it only took me about four hours for both, not counting drying time for coating and paint. This method can be used to make any type of throne by changing fabric, decorations, and paint color. For instance, if you need an **African Throne,** you would use earth tones and decorate with raffia and feathers. For a **Medieval Throne,** you might want to go with heavier-looking decorations and darker colors. You can even make a fabulous **Santa Throne** in white fur and paint. You are only limited by your imagination.

Queen Crown

King Crown

Crowns

Crowns can be made of so many things, from the bottom of plastic bottles to felt hats. You will be trying to achieve a heavy look that isn't heavy and a crown that doesn't slip off the head. I've come up with a method to accomplish both. As with the thrones, we will be going for a bolder look for the king and a more delicate look for the queen.

I coated two short-crowned, plastic top hats with Sculptural Arts Coating to use as the bases of my crowns, and let dry.

Making the Costume

1. Cut the brims off and the tops out of the top hats so you're left with a short round tube of coated plastic.

2. Turn the tubes upside down so the wider end is on top.

3. Cut out the crown points, leaving a band at the bottom of the tube.

4. Decorate the crowns with whatever you have. I used old beads, beaded trim, and some sequin appliques from a dress.

5. Cut the bill off a ball cap and glue the King's crown around the cap about an inch above the edge. Glue the Queen's crown to a plastic headband on both sides. Glue a piece of felt over where you attached the crown to the headband to help secure it.

6. Either spray paint the crowns with gold or use gold leaf paint. I used gold leaf. Paint inside and out.

7. Cut strips of fur long enough to go around the crown and wide enough to double. Fold and glue the strips in half lengthwise. Then glue them to the crowns. You'll notice I made the king's fur strip wider and glued it to the part of ball cap we left uncovered. Be sure not to glue over the adjustable closure in the back of the ball cap. Glue the fur above it so it hangs down over it. If you can't find Dalmatian fur, use white fur and a black marker.

8. I glued a few large fake rhinestones to the king's crown and more to the queen's crown. I thought she needed a bit more glitz.

As with the thrones, this method can be used to make whatever type of crown you need, from a plain **Medieval Circle Crown** to a fancy **English Crown.** You can use the crown from almost any hat and covert it very easily. By coating the plastic and the ball cap, the glue will adhere better and it will give your paint a more metallic finish.

If you have thrones and crowns, you'll need **Scepters.** Buy a thin dowel rod at the hardware store for about twenty cents. Paint it gold, or cover it with fabric and coat it. Add whatever you want at the end. You can use pipe cleaners for structure, cut something out of cardboard, use an old applique, or attach a large broach. Just glue something to the end of a gold stick and call it a scepter. (See King and Queen Scepters.)

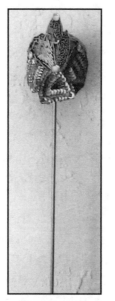

King Scepter

Queen Scepter

Chapter 17 Dinnerware

King Mug

Queen Goblet

Medieval Mug

While rummaging, watch for goblets, cheap candleholders, cups, even old teapots that can be converted into props for productions. It doesn't matter if they are glass, plastic, ceramic, or even paper as long as they are the right shape. And if you can find objects with designs on them, you are already ahead of the game. Most can be purchased for less than a dollar. By using metallic paints, converting these items to period dinnerware only takes a matter of minutes. I used Plasti-Kote brush-on Odds 'n' Ends Fast Dry Enamel. It comes in gold leaf, silver, pewter, copper, chrome, and other colors, and it will cover almost any surface. Although I'm sure the paint can be bought through craft shops and discount stores, I buy it at our local hardware store.

It is very easy to find old goblets and mugs at garage sales and thrift shops. They are inexpensive and easy to convert into a **King's Mug** or a **Queen's Goblet.**

It really doesn't matter what design is on the object because you'll be decorating and painting it. I chose a milk-white goblet and a mug that looked like it came from an Oktoberfest to use as my base. Wash them well and let them dry. Coat them with Sculptural Arts Coating. Decorate with trim, beads, or whatever you desire, and spray paint. You can paint them gold, silver, white, or pewter, depending on the look you're going for. If you want more color, simply glue fake jewels and trim on or create the appearance of jewels by using fabric paint. Because you coated the object, the glue and fabric paint will adhere better. (See Queen Goblet and King Mug.)

If you need a big, **Heavy-Looking Mug** for the medieval period, pewter paint will work best. It has that dark gray metallic appearance. I found a brown ceramic mug, glued some beads from a necklace around it and painted it with pewter. (See Medieval Mug.)

A clear glass **Goblet,** painted with copper, would work well if a character wants to appear to be drinking poison in a Shakespeare play. (See Copper Goblet.)

Copper Goblet

Doing an English tea for your play? Can't find a **Silver Teapot** and **Cups** or **Plates?** I've found the chrome paint gives a wonderful appearance of silver. I located a ceramic teapot with a bamboo handle, glass cups from a punch bowl set, and a paper plate. I coated them with chrome paint, and I think they look like silver. The paint also gives the appearance of weight. **Candlesticks** can be done the same way. If you need them for a table or for your heroine to carry down a spooky hallway, painting and adding decoration to a pair of cheap, plastic candlesticks make all the difference. I decorated mine for the silver look. (See Teapot, Cup, Plate, and Candlesticks.)

Teapot, Cup, Plate, and Candlesticks

Remember in those pirate productions where they find the pile of gold and jewels? I thought of that when I found a **Handled Vase** made of woven straw. So many shapes of baskets and vases are made from straw. These items are cheap, but they take a bit more work to convert. I coated my vase with strips of newspaper and Sculptural Arts Coating, covering inside the lip, and let it dry. I then painted it with gold leaf to give it that beaten gold look. Once you've done this, you'll never look at straw the same way. By putting a heavy coat of Sculptural Arts Coating on it — heavy enough to make it smooth — and painting it white, this vase would have worked well for a Greek play — perhaps a water girl might carry it. Because it's so lightweight, the vase could even be attached to a headpiece to look as if the wearer is carrying it on his or her head. (See Beaten Gold Vase.)

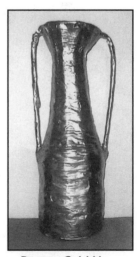

Beaten Gold Vase

Wine Bottle

In the past, **Wine Bottles** were made of animal skin, wood, anything that would hold liquid. If you're lucky, you can find an empty wine bottle in the shape you want. In a hurry, I found a vase I thought would work. I covered it with strips of suede cloth and twine, made three rings around it from felt, added a cork from the hardware store and coated it with Sculptural Arts Coating to give it the look of skin. (See Wine Bottle.)

Before you begin dinnerware, consider the time period you need it for. Before painting, decide if you need extra objects glued on. It doesn't matter what color they are because the paint will cover them. After painting, you can use fabric paint, jewelry, plastic jewels from old beaded curtains, even buttons to decorate.

If you must actually drink from a mug, goblet, or cup, don't use Sculptural Arts Coating on it. If you're playing pretend, the coating can serve you in two ways: It will make the object easier to paint and less likely to break. When I use paper plates, I normally coat two, press them together, coat the outside, then paint them. This gives the finished prop more weight and prevents tearing. With this method, you'll be surprised how little money and time is spent making dinnerware props, and they look good.

Chapter 18 Lamps

Some of the stranger props I've been asked to make are period lamps. It's quite easy to find old lamps at garage sales and in thrift stores, make a few changes, and turn them into period lamps.

I've chosen lamps from the 1930s. For the **Floor Lamp,** locate an old metal floor lamp. It doesn't matter what condition the shade is in, or even if the lamp has a shade. You can use one from another lamp. After all, it just sits on top. I found one with a terrible shade.

I had a white dress with a layered white flounce around the bottom. It would be the perfect size. I cut the flounce off, glued it to the top of the shade, and glued blue lace trim around the top. I glued long white fringe to the bottom and another strip of lace at the top of the fringe. It took me all of ten minutes to convert the lamp. (See Floor Lamp.)

The same thing can be accomplished with a **Table Lamp.** I covered mine with a piece of brown and white curtain fabric and glued gold fringe at the top and around the bottom of the shade. If you can't find the base you want and the lamp doesn't actually have to work, use a vase and set the shade on top. Again, fast, cheap, and easy. (See Table Lamp.)

Floor Lamp

Floor Lamp
Original Dress

Table Lamp

Section IV

Illusion Costumes

Chapter 19 **Illusions**

Webster defines an illusion as a misleading image presented to the vision. That describes most of my costumes, but some more than others. My illusion costumes range from simple to elaborate and the cost is in tune with how fancy or complicated the costume is and the amount of materials needed.

Fat Witch Illusion

In recent years, a popular costume has been the fat body costume. You can purchase these fat bodies from costume companies, but they are flesh-colored nylon with stuffing. Talk about hot and hard to wear — and expensive! When a female customer asked if I could design her a fat witch, I had to put my thinking cap on. It had to be cool, comfortable, but still give the illusion of weight.

Fat Witch Illusion

My answer came from an old hoop skirt and a plastic butt I already had on hand.

Creating the Illusion

1. Remove the drawstring from the waist of the hoop skirt.

2. Glue the ends of the waistband together and add straps made of pieces of old suspenders to bring the waist of the hoop skirt up to just under the chest.

3. Using a pair of pliers, pinch the boning of the first hoop to give the appearance of a waist — a big waist.

4. Cut the bottom of the skirt out of a long black dress and glue it on the waist.

5. After coating the plastic butt with Sculptural Arts Coating, let it dry and glue it directly to the hoop skirt above the waist. The butt is now a bust.

6. Cover the top with fabric left over from the black dress, making sure the upper chest is covered with lace so the "bust" shows through.

7. Glue red sequin trim around the waist to look like a belt, and glue a black cape to the back at the top edge of the hoop skirt.

8. Glue a piece of black boa around the top edge above the bust and over the wide suspender straps.

9. Add a witch's hat and long red and white socks, and you have a fat witch.

You may want to put a coat of Sculptural Arts Coating on the inside of the hoop skirt. This will keep it from tearing or fraying. Because the costume will be worn over clothes, you will only need to spot clean it.

Miss Piggy Illusion

One lady who wore the fat witch decided she'd like to have a **Miss Piggy** costume done in the same manner. The only difference is it's pink, and I used maribu at the neckline and over the straps. There is no cape.

This illusion is cool, easy to wear, and can even be worn by a man by adding a mask. (See Miss Piggy Illusion.)

Cousin Itt Illusion

Cousin Itt Illusion

A couple wanted to have a theme wedding based on the Addams Family, and Cousin Itt would be the ring bearer. Cousin Itt was no more than a pile of hair with glasses and a hat. The simplest way to make the costume was with yarn. It could have been made from fake fur, but I really don't think it would have looked as good. For one thing, it's hard to find the brown color I needed in fur that long.

Where to begin? I found a man's large felt hat with a rounded crown. This hat was large enough to fit over the eyes of the wearer. Perfect.

Creating the Illusion

1. Cut the brim off the man's black felt hat. Attach a piece of elastic to the crown. The elastic should fit snuggly under the chin.

2. Cut eyeholes where needed and apply Sculptural Arts Coating to the outside of the hat. Let dry.

3. Cut long lengths of brown yarn. Glue them into sections of brown fabric that are long enough to fit around the hat. Begin gluing on the lengths of fabric and yarn at the bottom edge of the hat and keep layering until you get to the top. Make sure one layer is glued directly above the eyeholes, but not across them. Trim the yarn around the eyeholes and head to make it look like shorter hair around the head.

4. Glue a pair of sunglasses over the eyes. Make a spider web design from fabric paint on a derby and glue the derby to the top of the head.

Although this costume will take a lot of yarn, I think the look will be worth it in the end. The person who wore it tape-recorded his voice on a small recorder, hung the recorder around his neck under the costume, and played the tape backward to make himself sound like Cousin Itt. He wore a brown shirt, pants, and gloves beneath the costume. Cousin Itt was a hit.

> **T I P**
>
> When you need to cut a lot of yarn, find an object that is the same length as the yarn you need and wrap the yarn around and around it, then cut the yarn at both ends. That way cutting the yarn will take very little time. I used a metal clothes rack attached to the wall.

Big Hat Illusion

If you haven't seen the Big Hat Costume, it is funny. My big hat was made of foam — 2" for the crown and 4" for the brim. It had to be made large enough to fit over the wearer's shoulders.

Big Hat Illusion

Creating the Illusion

1. Wrap the foam around the person who will wear the costume so you can make sure it's big enough. Cut the foam and cover it with black short nap fur. Glue the ends together to form the crown of the hat.

2. Cut a circle of foam to put on the top of the hat and glue on fur. Glue to the crown piece.

3. Cut a rectangle out of the side of the hat where the eyes are located and glue black mesh over it. I used four layers of black netting. This way the wearer can see out, but people can't see in. Glue strips of black felt around the edge of the netting to hold it in place. If you glue it on the outside, do it before you glue the black fur on. I attached the netting to the inside.

4. Cut a large circle of 4" foam for the brim. Set the crown piece in the center of the brim circle and, with a white chalk pencil, mark where to cut the opening where you will attach it. Cut out the marked areas.

5. Cover the brim with black fur. Glue the crown to the brim and glue a red fur band around where the two pieces meet.

The face is built on a flesh-colored leotard. The eyelids and nose are made of 1/2" foam covered with pink fur and glued directly to the leotard. The eyelashes and eyebrows are strips of black fur. The big lips and bow tie are made of foam with red fur glued on. This costume is completely washable as long as you use cold water and hang it to dry.

The hat will sit just above the "eyes," and by putting your hands on your hips, you will give the illusion of large ears. If you find the hat is too wobbly, add some thick foam inside the back to stabilize it. We didn't have that problem.

Foam is not cheap, but I was able to find my 4" foam at a yard sale — it had been used with a camping bed. The 2" foam was purchased from a store. Look to a dancewear shop if you can't find a flesh-colored leotard. If you don't make this costume with a full-length leotard, you'll want to wear tights. This method can be used to make all manner of dancing cigarette packs, do a big calypso fruit hat, and more. You are only limited by your imagination.

Aussie Annie and Lulu Illusion

Aussie Annie and Lulu Illusion

I must tell you, the Aussie Annie and Lulu costume is one of my personal favorites. I had so much fun making it. Believe me when I say it looks more difficult than it was. Because of the feathers used, this was a much more costly illusion.

The dress was a flared maternity top decorated with sequin trim and flowers. I added an old cowboy hat, red braided wig, and some makeup to finish the costume. Aussie Annie now resides in a shop in Maryland.

Creating the Illusion

1. You'll need three pillows filled with polyester fiberfill stuffing to start. Cut one in half and glue the cut ends closed.

2. Lay the full pillows parallel to each other and glue one of the half pillows across the ends of both to form the breast of the bird. Push the other end of each pillow to a point and glue.

3. Glue the two points together to form the back of the ostrich body. Glue the other half pillow on top of the point in back, making it as flat as possible. The wearer's body should fit in the circle of pillows.

4. Wrap a piece of wire around the side of each full pillow and connect the pillows in the back with another piece of wire. I used clothesline wire.

5. Cut the neck and head out of a piece of thick foam. Slice it lengthwise about halfway through and glue a piece of wire in the slice. Pull the foot and leg from a pair of tights over the foam. The toe will be the beak and the heel will be the top of the head. Tie the end closed.

6. Glue the neck inside the front of the circle of pillows, right behind where you attached the half pillow. Bring the full pillows together behind the neck and glue them to secure the neck.

7. Coat the neck and head with Sculptural Arts Coating and let dry.

8. Attach a pair of wide suspenders to the wires on each side and in the back to hold the bird body on.

9. Coat the outside of the pillows with Sculptural Arts Coating, leaving the inside soft and natural. Let dry.

10. Starting at the back, glue on natural-colored ostrich tail feathers and leave them hanging down.

11. Starting from the bottom, glue strings of black coque feathers to the sides and tops of the pillows in layers. Glue white coque feathers around the neck.

12. Make the bulging eyes with halves of a white plastic egg. Glue fabric eyelids and big lashes on. The beak is coated gold fabric. I added a small, feathered hat with a sash tie. The harness is made of gold Christmas beads.

13. To make the bird legs, manipulate a pair of extra-long gray tights to make them look like two toes, glue the toes in place, and stuff them with fiberfill. The toenails are black fabric with shiny black fabric paint over it.

14. To make the fake legs hanging off the front, stuff a pair of long, red and white clown socks and tie them to a belt that fits the wearer's waist. The boots were too heavy, so I cut the soles out, replaced them with felt and trimmed them with sequin trim before I glued them to the fake legs.

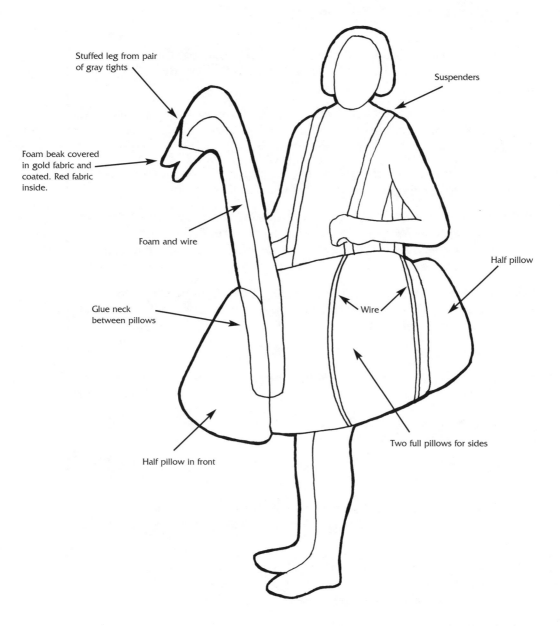

Stuffed leg from pair
of gray tights

Suspenders

Foam beak covered
in gold fabric and
coated. Red fabric
inside.

Foam and wire

Half pillow

Glue neck
between pillows

Wire

Half pillow in front

Two full pillows for sides

Aussie Annie and Lulu Sketch #1

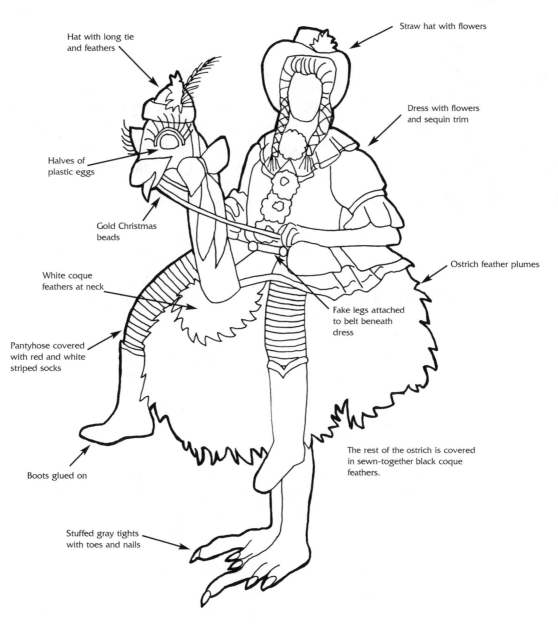

Hat with long tie
and feathers

Straw hat with flowers

Halves of
plastic eggs

Dress with flowers
and sequin trim

Gold Christmas
beads

Ostrich feather plumes

White coque
feathers at neck

Fake legs attached
to belt beneath
dress

Pantyhose covered
with red and white
striped socks

The rest of the ostrich is covered
in sewn-together black coque
feathers.

Boots glued on

Stuffed gray tights
with toes and nails

Aussie Annie and Lulu Sketch #2

Cardinal Queen

Cardinal Queen

The same method I used for Aussie Annie and Lulu worked well for me when I needed an illusion that looked like a queen riding a cardinal for the Mrs. Illinois Pageant. It was a bit different, but the same idea.

Creating the Illusion

1. Start with two queen-size pillows filled with polyester fiberfill. Glue the ends together for the front, and push and glue each pillow into a point at the back. Glue the points together.

2. Cut the shape of the cardinal's head out of thick foam and cover with red fur. Glue the head directly to the pillows, leaving a strip long enough to glue inside the pillows for a more secure hold. Coat the outside of the pillows and the fur-covered head with Sculptural Arts Coating and let dry.

3. Glue black fur on the face and chest. Cover the beak with gold fabric and coat it.

4. Wrap a piece of wire around the side of each pillow and wrap another piece around both in the back to connect them. Attach wide white suspenders to the wires in the front and back to hold the bird body up. I used clothesline wire.

5. Glue red fur on the sides of both pillows and glue wings cut from foam over it. This will save you from having to use so many feathers.

6. Starting at the tail, attach long red feather plumes and leave them hanging down for the tail. Glue strips of sewn-together red coque feathers to cover the wings and breast.

7. I used gold tights for the bird legs, gluing them at the toe to create the appearance of three toes.

8. For the queen's legs, I stuffed a pair of natural-colored hose, coated them, and glued a pair of gold shoes to each foot. They are tied to a belt at the top. The belt is hidden under the dress.

On this costume, one leg is crossed over the bird body so both legs hang down one side. I used a white gown with no waist to drape over the legs and added a cape made from the skirt of another dress. I adorned the cape with a white fur collar and gold trim. I made the crown from a hat and trimmed with white and gold. The last thing I did was make a harness for the bird using gold trim.

Queen Cardinal made it to the Mrs. Illinois Pageant. Although the person did not win the title, she got high points for her costume.

There are pretty birds, and some not-so-pretty birds. I created an illusion costume that looked like a **Desert Survivor** with a vulture riding on the backpack. The backpack was actually a lightweight wooden crate covered with tan desert fabric, ragged as if from wear, and attached to straps from a real backpack. I cut the body of the vulture from a chunk of foam, the wings from thin foam. The tail, body, and outer wings are covered with black fur and black feather plumes. The head was the bottom of one leg of a child's size pair of tights. I added some makeup and coated it, made the beak and eyes with black fabric paint, and glued white maribu around the neck. The flesh in the mouth is latex. (See Vulture Illusion.)

Vulture Illusion

> **TIP**
> When cutting foam, use an electric knife. It saves time and gives you a cleaner edge.
> If you rub a dryer sheet on your clothes before working with foam it won't stick all over your clothes.

Head-on-a-Platter Illusion

My job as a costumer wasn't always pretty. I did a lot of illusions for haunted houses. One of my more unusual ones was the ghoul carrying a man's head on a platter. That's not that unusual, but the head on the platter was the wearer.

The wearer (i.e., the head on the platter) should either wear a mask or paint his face with makeup if he has the ability. If you use a mask, be sure it's in keeping with the illusion. You might think this costume can only be used for horror, but you could also use it in a production by changing the mask and robe on the back. Think about it.

Be sure the body behind the wearer will stand up well. The hands attached to the platter help hold it forward.

Head-on-a-Platter Illusion

Creating the Illusion

1. Have the wearer lie down on a piece of thick foam and, with a Magic Marker, draw around his or her head and arms (including the hands), down to the waist. Cut the foam body out. As you get closer to the waist, taper the foam to half the width.

2. Glue the foam body to a back belt — one that closes in the front with Velcro and has straps — so the body stands up behind the wearer.

3. Stuff a pair of gloves and glue them to the ends of the arms.

4. Slice the head down the center almost to the neck and glue in another piece of foam perpendicularly.

5. Find the largest size ghoul robe of the heaviest fabric you can. Cut a hole in the chest and sew a piece of elastic around the hole big enough for the wearer's head to go through. Glue a ghoul head with eyes onto the head of the foam body and glue the hood of the robe around it so it drapes over the forehead and sides a bit.

6. Make a platter out of foam, cutting a hole the size of the wearer's neck in the center. Make some slits around the neck opening so it will be easy to slip over the head. Coat and paint the platter silver.

7. Using yarn, fabric paint, and fake blood, make it look like a bloody mess on the platter.

8. Attach the gloves to the platter with heavy duty Velcro. The arms will bend because they are foam.

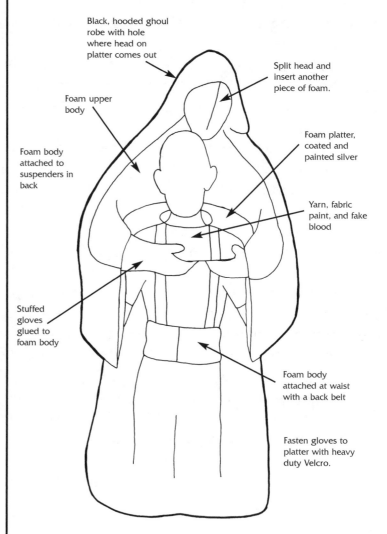

Black, hooded ghoul robe with hole where head on platter comes out

Foam upper body

Split head and insert another piece of foam.

Foam platter, coated and painted silver

Foam body attached to suspenders in back

Yarn, fabric paint, and fake blood

Stuffed gloves glued to foam body

Foam body attached at waist with a back belt

Fasten gloves to platter with heavy duty Velcro.

Head-on-a-Platter Illusion

Woman Riding Spider Illusion

I have a terrible fear of spiders, and one night I had a nightmare in which a woman riding a huge, hairy-legged spider was chasing me. Ever the vigilant costumer, when I awakened, I thought, *That would make a great costume.* I sketched it in the wee hours of the morning. Building the costume would be another cup of tea.

Woman Riding Spider Illusion

Creating the Illusion

1. Start with a hoop skirt and an evening gown with a black full skirt. The one I used was black velveteen.

2. Cut the skirt away from the bodice of the evening gown and glue the edge under. Make several loops from excess fabric and attach them to the waist with safety pins. Pinch the heads of the pins and glue excess fabric from the dress over them. Run a wide, leather belt through the loops. Make sure it is sturdy. The skirt should now hang around the hips.

3. Remove the drawstring from the waist of the hoop skirt. Glue the ends together. Replace the boning in the hoop skirt with flat spring wire. Use duct tape to connect the ends of the wire. Glue the waist of the hoop skirt inside the waist of the black skirt now hanging from the hips.

4. To make the legs, cut eight strips of 6" foam, each eight feet long. Slice them down the center lengthways, halfway through, and glue wire inside. I used clothesline wire.

5. Cut eight slits in the black skirt where you wish to attach the legs, and cut eight more slits in the hoop skirt at corresponding spots. The slits should be cut above the first wire hoop.

6. Bring the foam legs through the two layers of skirts and inside the wire hoop. Attach them to the inside of the wire hoop and glue in place.

7. Glue the slits closed around the foam legs.

8. Use a round pillow filled with fiberfill to make the head. Glue black fabric on the pillow and glue the pillow directly to the front of the black skirt.

9. Coat the legs with Sculptural Arts Coating and wrap black boas around them. Let dry. It takes two black boas to cover a leg. You'll need sixteen.

10. Glue black and gold maribu at the bottom of the black skirt and to cover the head.

11. Cover a strip of foam with red satin and black sequin trim for the collar and glue it on where the head meets skirt.

12. Make eyes from two halves of a plastic egg, red sequin trim, and black fabric paint. The mouth is foam covered with red sequin trim. The harness is made of gold braided drapery ties.

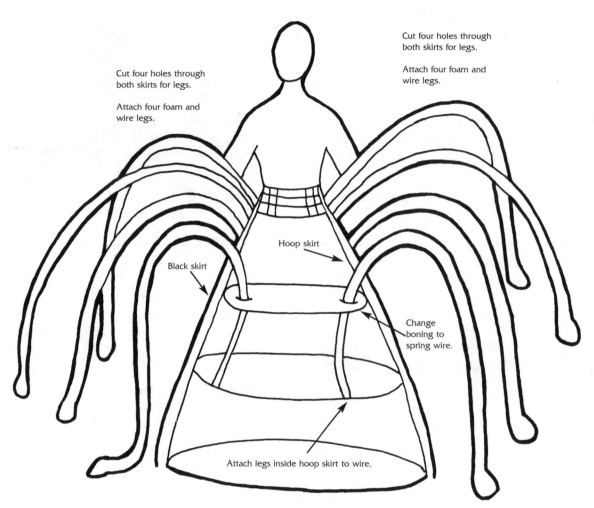

Cut four holes through
both skirts for legs.

Attach four foam and
wire legs.

Cut four holes through
both skirts for legs.

Attach four foam and
wire legs.

Hoop skirt

Black skirt

Change
boning to
spring wire.

Attach legs inside hoop skirt to wire.

Woman Riding a Spider Illusion Sketch #1

The black skirt is attached to a belt with loops so it hangs from
the hips. The waist of the hoop skirt is glued inside the black skirt.
Use duct tape to attach the wires together inside the hoop skirt.

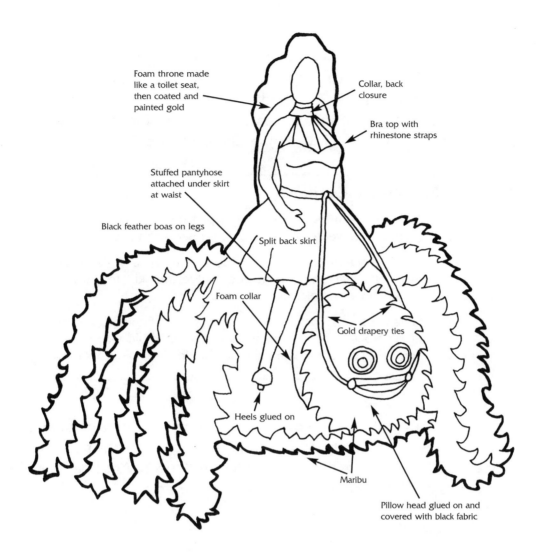

Foam throne made
like a toilet seat,
then coated and
painted gold

Collar, back
closure

Bra top with
rhinestone straps

Stuffed pantyhose
attached under skirt
at waist

Black feather boas on legs

Split back skirt

Foam collar

Gold drapery ties

Heels glued on

Maribu

Pillow head glued on and
covered with black fabric

Woman Riding a Spider Illusion Sketch #2

Because of the way the body of the spider is made, the legs can be bent for the desired look, and when the wearer walks, it really looks like the spider legs are moving. Because the head is attached to the movable skirt fabric, it can be moved with the reins.

Although I initially chose a showgirl look for the costume I wore with the spider illusion, I later made other costumes to wear with it. At Halloween a witch would be appropriate. For a sci-fi event, an alien costume can be worn. Even a wizard works well. But my original costume was called "Queen Arachna" and looked like a showgirl. Well, when you have a queen, you need a throne.

To give the appearance that the queen is sitting on a throne, I made one out of foam and wire. It actually looked like a toilet seat, big enough to fit over the head and shoulders of the wearer and sit at the hip. I decorated it with gold beads, coated it with Sculptural Arts Coating, and gold leafed it. It was lightweight and did the job.

Making the Costume

1. Make the fake legs by stuffing a pair of panty hose and attaching them at the wearer's waist. Glue on heels to the feet.

2. To cover where the fake legs are attached, cut a flared skirt off a dress and leave one seam open. Glue the skirt to the inside of a waistband with Velcro closure in the back.

3. Enhance a black strapless bra with lines of rhinestones and gold glitter fabric paint to make the top. I added a black choker necklace. See the Hats and Headpieces section for the spider web hat.

You might think this costume would be hard to take anywhere, but you simply lay the body down and fold the legs into it. The problem with wearing it is getting through doorways. Queen Arachna does best in parades and trade shows, or at an outside party.

Clown Car Illusion

Clown Car Illusion

Clown car illusions can be made easily with a cardboard box covered in felt and coated, or they can be more fancy. For a clown parade, I chose to go fancy. I wanted more rounded lines, so I built my box with 2" foam. Then I broke out that Sculptural Arts Coating. It took a lot to cover the car. The problem was that the car would be too heavy to wear on the shoulders in a parade. I discovered the solution.

I added an emblem on the side, glued on a hood ornament, and used felt and paint to make the grill. Last, I attached a horn to the driver's side and added a dog hanging out the back, dressed like the wearer and secured with Velcro so he could be removed and cleaned.

Creating the Illusion

1. Cut four pieces of 2" foam as long as you want the car. Cut two pieces as wide as you want the car. Glue the pieces together to make a rectangular box with the top and bottom open.

2. To make the hood, bend a piece of foam across the top of the box in the front and glue it to both sides. Glue a small upside down U-shaped piece from the bottom of the front to the hood.

3. Glue a square piece of foam across the back to look like a trundle seat, making sure to leave plenty of room for the wearer. Make the back seat rests by bending a piece of foam over and gluing it.

4. Glue three strips of foam together to make a windshield frame and glue it to the front behind the hood. Glue white sheer fabric on from the inside for a windshield.

5. Attach a piece of wire in two places on either side of the car — wrap one end where the windshield meets the car frame, and another where the edge of the car door might be. Leave the wire long enough to attach to a back belt for the wearer.

6. Cover the entire car frame with black felt and coat with Sculptural Arts Coating. Let dry.

7. Cover the seats in purple and gold fabric and coat.

8. Build a frame of 2x2" wood. Drill holes in the bottom to add casters from an office chair. You can build the frame from PVC pipe and joints the same way. (See pattern.)

9. Set the car on the frame.

10. Cut five circles of foam large enough for tires. Coat and paint them with chrome paint. Cut wide strips of black felt. Roll each into a tube and fill it with fiberfill. Glue the ends together, coat, and glue the tubes to the tires. Make spokes from silver trim or fabric paint.

11. Attach the tires to the car body. I attached mine with heavy, wide strips of Velcro, but you can glue them directly to the body. Glue the extra tire to the back.

12. Make two headlights from the ends of plastic bottles and a foam cone. Cover and coat. Glue them on.

13. Make fenders of foam, cover and coat them, and glue them on above the wheels

The clown costume consisted of a lab coat dyed tan, a red silk scarf, a Willie Richardson mask, goggles, and a flyer's hat with red clown wig attached.

The car didn't quite meet the floor and I didn't want the wearer's shoes to show, so I glued red fringe along both sides of the bottom.

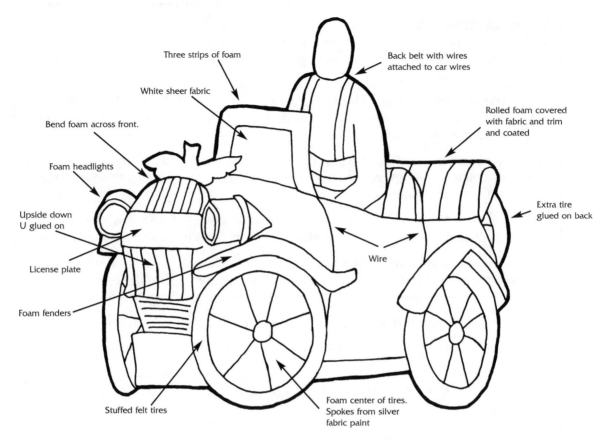

Three strips of foam

White sheer fabric

Bend foam across front.

Foam headlights

Upside down
U glued on

License plate

Foam fenders

Back belt with wires
attached to car wires

Rolled foam covered
with fabric and trim
and coated

Extra tire
glued on back

Wire

Stuffed felt tires

Foam center of tires.
Spokes from silver
fabric paint

Costume covers upper body. Car is covered in black felt and coated.

Clown Car Illusion

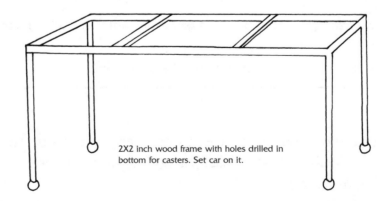

2X2 inch wood frame with holes drilled in
bottom for casters. Set car on it.

References

Accessories, Props
Caufield's Novelties
1006 West Main Street
Louisville, KY 40202
(502) 583-0636

Cheaper Costume Accessories
Oriental Trading Co.
4206 S. 108th St.
Omaha, NE 68137
(402) 331-5511
(800) 228-2269

Costumes, Accessories, Masks, Props
Morris Costumes
3108 Monroe Road
Charlotte, NC 28205
(704) 332-3304

Rubies Costumes
One Rubie Plaza
Richmond Hills, NY 11418
(718) 846-1008

Fabric, Trim
Foust Textiles
608 Canterbury Rd.
Kings Mountain, NC 28086
(800) 258-9816

Feathers
Zucker Feather Products
28419 Hwy 87
California, MO 65018
(573) 796-2183

Glue Guns, Glue
Red Hill Adhesives
P.O. Box 4234
Gettysburg, PA 17325
(717) 337-3038
(800) 822-4003

Period Accessories, Props
Junk for Joy
3314 West Magnolia Blvd
Burbank, CA 91505
(818) 569-4903

Sculpting or Coating Supplies
Sculptural Arts Coating, Inc.
501 Guilford Ave.
Greensboro, NC 27401
(336) 379-7651
(800) 743-0379
www.sculpturalarts.com

Slips
Sweetheart Slips
14837 NE 20 Ave
North Miami, FL 33181
(305) 919-7737
(800) 227-7547

Unique Latex Masks
M.A.S.K.S.
W.P. Richardson
1 West 24th Street
Baltimore, MD 21218
(410) 243-0010

Wigs
Lacey Costume Wig
318 W 39th St, 10th Floor
New York, NY 10018
(212) 695-1996
(800) 562-9911

Many of the companies listed are now online. If you are interested, check the Internet for more information.

Index

About the Author

A single mother for many years, Barb Rogers haunted thrift shops, rummage sales, and auctions in the hope of finding old clothes that could be converted into costumes and sold. Not a seamstress, unable to use a pattern, and without a sewing machine, she developed her own unique way of designing costumes.

She returned to school and earned a bachelor's degree from Eastern Illinois University, where she studied psychology and communications. But her first love remained costuming.

Broadway Bazaar Costumes was born in one upstairs room on the main street of Mattoon, Illinois, with 130 costumes and Ms. Roger's burning desire to succeed. Within five years, it had grown to fifteen rooms of fun, fabulous, flamboyant costumes.

As a member of the National Costumers Association, Barb attended national conventions, competed with costumers from all over the United States, and won many awards. After ten years in business, Ms. Rogers was brought down by a serious illness. The shop was leased, then sold.

Always the survivor and eternal optimist, but unable to continue running a shop, Ms. Rogers found her second love: writing. Barb, her husband, Junior, and two dogs, Sammi and Georgie, relocated to a small mountain community in Arizona, where she could heal and write. In addition to working on her costume books, Barb has developed a fortune-telling kit, *Native American Glyphs,* and has aspirations of becoming a novelist. Despite these new activities, costuming will forever be in her blood.

Barb Rogers

Order Form

Meriwether Publishing Ltd.
PO Box 7710
Colorado Springs CO 80933-7710
Phone: 800-937-5297 Fax: 719-594-9916
Website: www.meriwether.com

Please send me the following books:

_____ **Costumes, Accessories, Props and** $19.95
Stage Illusions Made Easy #BK-B279
by Barb Rogers
How to make costumes, accessories, props and stage illusions

_____ **Instant Period Costumes #BK-B244** $19.95
by Barb Rogers
How to make classic costumes from cast-off clothing

_____ **Costuming Made Easy #BK-B229** $19.95
by Barb Rogers
How to make theatrical costumes from cast-off clothing

_____ **Elegantly Frugal Costumes #BK-B125** $15.95
by Shirley Dearing
A do-it-yourself costume maker's guide

_____ **Broadway Costumes on a Budget #BK-B166** $15.95
by Janet Litherland and Sue McAnally
Big-time ideas for amateur producers

_____ **Self-Supporting Scenery #BK-B105** $15.95
by James Hull Miller
A scenic workbook for the open stage

_____ **Stagecraft I #BK-B116** $19.95
by William H. Lord
A complete guide to backstage work

**These and other fine Meriwether Publishing books are available at your
local bookstore or direct from the publisher. Prices subject to change
without notice. Check our website or call for current prices.**

Name: _____ e-mail: _____

Organization name: _____

Address: _____

City: _____ State: _____

Zip: _____ Phone: _____

❑ **Check enclosed**
❑ **Visa / MasterCard / Discover #** _____

Signature: _____   *Expiration*
date: _____

(required for credit card orders)

Colorado residents: Please add 3% sales tax.
Shipping: Include $3.95 for the first book and 75¢ for each additional book ordered.

❑ *Please send me a copy of your complete catalog of books and plays.*

Order Form

Meriwether Publishing Ltd.
PO Box 7710
Colorado Springs CO 80933-7710
Phone: 800-937-5297 Fax: 719-594-9916
Website: www.meriwether.com

Please send me the following books:

_____ **Costumes, Accessories, Props and**   **$19.95**
Stage Illusions Made Easy #BK-B279
by Barb Rogers
How to make costumes, accessories, props and stage illusions

_____ **Instant Period Costumes #BK-B244**   **$19.95**
by Barb Rogers
How to make classic costumes from cast-off clothing

_____ **Costuming Made Easy #BK-B229**   **$19.95**
by Barb Rogers
How to make theatrical costumes from cast-off clothing

_____ **Elegantly Frugal Costumes #BK-B125**   **$15.95**
by Shirley Dearing
A do-it-yourself costume maker's guide

_____ **Broadway Costumes on a Budget #BK-B166**   **$15.95**
by Janet Litherland and Sue McAnally
Big-time ideas for amateur producers

_____ **Self-Supporting Scenery #BK-B105**   **$15.95**
by James Hull Miller
A scenic workbook for the open stage

_____ **Stagecraft I #BK-B116**   **$19.95**
by William H. Lord
A complete guide to backstage work

These and other fine Meriwether Publishing books are available at your local bookstore or direct from the publisher. Prices subject to change without notice. Check our website or call for current prices.

Name: _____ e-mail: _____

Organization name: _____

Address: _____

City: _____ State: _____

Zip: _____ Phone: _____

❑ **Check enclosed**
❑ **Visa / MasterCard / Discover #** _____

                                              Expiration
Signature: _____ *date:* _____
       (required for credit card orders)

Colorado residents: Please add 3% sales tax.
Shipping: Include $3.95 for the first book and 75¢ for each additional book ordered.

❑ *Please send me a copy of your complete catalog of books and plays.*